THE ESTABLISH- MENT

vs.

THE PEOPLE

IS A NEW POPULIST REVOLT ON THE WAY?

RICHARD A. VIGUERIE

REGNERY GATEWAY, INC.
Chicago, Ill.

For information address:

Regnery Gateway, Inc.
360 West Superior Street
Chicago, Illinois 60610
(312) 346-6646

First Edition, November, 1983

ISBN: 0-89526-608-3
Library of Congress Catalog Card No.: 83-63103

Printed in the United States of America

Dedication

This book is lovingly dedicated to my wife, Elaine, and our three children, Reneé, Michelle, and Ryan, for their strong support, faith, patience and understanding.

For those who choose to participate in the political arena, hard work is usually accompanied by feelings of satisfaction and fulfillment, and sometimes even fame.

But a person's participation in politics can be hard on his or her family, which must bear extra burdens and hardships.

For Elaine, there are children to raise, without the amount of help that most husbands can give. There are far too many telephone calls saying *I can't talk long, I'm in a meeting, just want to let you know I'll be late for supper*. And there are far too many nights and weekends and vacations when her husband just "can't get away from his job."

And the children are young for such a short time, it's easy to feel that they have been shortchanged.

But whenever I begin to doubt whether it's all worth it, I think about the many people who have made far, far greater sacrifices to the cause of freedom. With freedom comes responsibility. In the long run, it's the children (and their children, and theirs) for whom the sacrifices are made.

May they live in a world at least as free as the one previous generations left to us.

Acknowledgments

This book was shaped by many years of working with individuals across the country who seek political power only so that they can return it to the people. My sincere thanks to all of them.

Many people worked long and hard to make this book possible, typing, proofreading, researching through the night. It would be impossible for me to express fully my appreciation to them:

For managing what became known around the office as "that darn book," Linda Hedden and Bob Siegrist, and most especially, John Pucciano;

For his comments and suggestions, Howard Phillips;

For help with typing and related chores, Suzanne Yerks, Alvis Barbour, Tammy Beach, Diane Erickson, Karen Ferguson, Valerie Unser, Patti Hartis, Susan Tarnowsky, Scottie Heffner, Joan Kear, Betty Kenyon, Karen Demcsak, and Lisa McCarty, and especially Nancy Smith, Dottie Bradbury, Jill McBurney, Kathy Meenan, Pam Whitecotton, and Tammy Martin;

For help with word processing, Brenda Welch, Mike Gianino, and Chuck Gardner;

For help with typesetting, Terry Nilan and VIP Systems, Inc.;

For research, Rick LaMountain, Donna Ford, Derek Leaberry, and Garland McCoy;

For their ideas and input, Connie Marshner, Pat McGuigan, John McClaughry and Brien Benson;

For helping me find the right words, Steven Allen, Lee Edwards and Charlie Reese.

Table of Contents

Foreword

I spent months thinking of a title for this book. Finally, with time running out, I decided upon a title. Not particularly because I like the one I selected better than some others—but simply because John Pucciano, my Vice President in charge of publishing this book, insisted one Friday when I left the office that Monday morning I must give him a title for my book.

I thought I would share with you some other book titles I considered:

- The Case Against The Establishment
- Has the Establishment (Elite) Ruined America?
- Has the Establishment (Elite) Destroyed America?
- How the Big Boys did it to us
- A New Populist Manifesto
- The New Populism
- The Establishment is Bankrupt
- Who Messed up America?
- Who Ruined America?
- Who's Ruining Your Life?
- Who's Running Your Life?
- Conscience of a Populist
- How The Elite Stole America
- The Unrepresented Majority
- How 1 percent rules 99 percent
- Failed Leadership
- They Led, They Failed

"I consider myself a populist which I define as optimism about people and their willingness to respond to economic incentives as well as their ability to best control their own and their families' destinies."
—CONGRESSMAN JACK KEMP

"The populist movement in this country is held together by that strong moral fiber spun at the birth of this Nation. It speaks from the very soul of this country. It is what this country was and can be again."
—REV. JERRY FALWELL

"Regretfully a small elite has often frustrated the will of the majority of the American people. Will the populist revolt be necessary to restore the voice of the people?"
—DR. PAT ROBERTSON

"Today populism is the movement to restore the people's rights and prerogatives that our founding fathers had in mind in the first place."
—SENATOR WILLIAM ARMSTRONG

1 / The Power of the Elite

Today it is difficult to find leaders who are independent of the forces that have brought us our problems—the Congress, the bureaucracy, the lobbyists, big business and big labor.

If America is to survive and go forward, this must change. And it will change only when the American people vote for a leadership that is not part of the entrenched Washington establishment; leaders that will not be fettered by old commitments and friendships, that will be free to turn to the people for answers instead of to the federal bureaucracy.

—Reagan campaign brochure, 1976

For years, the American people have sought a leader who shared their values and their experiences. It is still true today. They want someone who can be comfortable in the presence of people from the highest levels of society but who, at heart, is still a farmer, small businessman, teacher, or salesman. They want someone who, unlike some politicians of humble origin, feels no inferiority in the company of rich men and self-styled intellectuals. They want someone who will sweep from the halls of power the bureaucrats who ridicule the beliefs and the lifestyle of ordinary Americans.

They want a leader who will champion the cause of the people against the establishment elite.

By the establishment elite I mean the class of persons with unusual access to the political process, whether gained through economic power or social status or through an old-boy network. It is characterized by the belief that people in general are not smart enough to manage their own affairs and, therefore, that the government should select intelligent, qualified persons to run society—preferably, so it seems, those bearing advanced degrees and other special credentials from eastern establishment institutions.

The elite tells people whether or not they must have airbags in their automobiles. The elite creates anti-poverty programs that specify how much of a poor person's imputed income may be spent on medicine, how much on food, and how much on a place to live (as, in effect, the Medicaid, food stamp, and public housing programs do).

It is elitist for the government, rather than the consumer, to decide which products will be sold and who will make a profit. Therefore, government subsidies which support business are elitist.

It is elitist to take money from the taxpayers who earn it and give it to bureaucrats to spend however *they* see fit. Therefore, high taxes are elitist.

The members of the establishment elite are part of the upper crust, either economically, socially, or as measured by how many university degrees they have. In the vast majority of cases, these members of the establishment have never got their hands dirty earning a living. They need not be rich; they may be professors, or bureaucrats, or TV commentators.

They are civil rights leaders more concerned about getting upper-class blacks into Harvard Medical School than making sure poor blacks can read or walk down neighborhood streets in safety. They are ministers more concerned with organizing protests against the Reagan Administration than with saving souls. They are television reporters who try to make the world conform to their own narrow leftwing ideology. They are Big Business, Big Banks, Big Media, Big Unions, Big Government, and their allies.

What they have in common is support for the concentration of power in the hands of a few. They oppose efforts to transfer decision-making from the federal level to the states, localities, and ultimately individual citizens. They reject the notion that decisions should be made at the level closest to the people and that, ideally, people should decide for themselves how to live as long as they do not violate the equal right of others to do so.

The elite fears any private institution strong enough to challenge the absolute authority of the central government. Private schools, churches, businesses, colleges, theaters, libraries, labor unions, and charitable organizations must be regulated into submission.

Sometimes this regulation is accomplished directly: for example, by a rule imposing hiring quotas on businesses. Sometimes it is accomplished by the withholding of a tax exemption, say, to a private school that does not comply with official doctrine. Sometimes it is more subtle, as when subsidies are available for charitable organizations that conduct programs approved by federal bureaucrats.

The establishment elite does not seek to impose a dictatorship on this country. Often its political power is translated from its economic and social power by means of persuasion and subtle intimidation.

Imagine yourself as an ambitious young journalist. Despite the high level of skill necessary to perform your job, you are basically a worker. Then you get an invitation to join the Council on Foreign Relations, the group that epitomizes America's foreign policy establishment. CFR is a very prestigious organization with membership by invitation only. It is very flattering to be invited to join.

You are in effect being asked to join the bosses' club. As a member, you will sit in a room of people who are not employees, but owners and top executives of important international corporations. Also present are top officials of the top universities, the largest newspapers, the television networks, and the book publishers. There, assembled in one place, are all the people an ambitious young journalist needs to please to succeed in his profession.

Here you will sit in a very clubby atmosphere, not with your peers, but with your superiors. You will get the inside scoop from some of the most respected names in the field of foreign policy. If what you write about an issue reflects what you were told by an expert at a CFR meeting, you will earn the approval of people who can make or break the careers of ambitious young journalists.

On the other hand, if what you write contradicts the expert, you may look foolish in the eyes of those important people. Why take the chance?

The Council on Foreign Relations does nothing more sinister than hiring academics to do studies and to present its members with special briefings by academics, government officials, and prominent businessmen. Its power, and the power of other elite organizations of the establishment, derives from its ability to establish its view as the proper view and contrary views as foolish. In this way opinion flows from the top down.

If the record of the establishment were one of brilliant success, one could understand our leaders' reliance upon it. But the record is one of repeated tragic failures.

After years of government controlled by the best and the brightest of Ivy League schools such as Harvard, Yale, and Princeton, what have we to show for it?

● Stalemate in Korea at a cost of 54,246 Americans killed and 103,284 wounded.

● Defeat in Vietnam, at a cost of 58,095 Americans killed and 155,419 wounded.

• Busing to achieve racial balance.

• The creation of a permanent class of tens of millions of welfare recipients.

• A Social Security system that owes 4.8 trillion dollars ($4,800,000,000,000) to working people.

• 1.6 trillion dollars ($1,600,000,000,000) owed in federal civilian, military and VA pensions.

• An increase of 140 percent in federal taxes in the last 23 years, even when adjusted for inflation.

• An inadequate national defense that encourages Soviet aggression around the world and which has, until Grenada, failed to free a single nation from communism, leaving one-and-a-half billion people in slavery.

• An international financial crisis caused by ill-advised loans by big banks to foreign, mostly anti-American, countries.

• A crime rate that has increased 274 percent since 1960.

• The highest "real" interest rates in American history.

• Declining test scores and increasing violence in the public schools.

• An epidemic of alcohol and drug abuse that has resulted in 10-12 million adult alcoholics, 3.3 million teenage alcoholics and the regular use of drugs by one-third of our nation's high-school seniors.

• An unemployment rate that has ranged up to 10.8 percent and is likely to remain so high that, according to the President's chief economic adviser, six or six-and-a-half percent unemployment should be considered full employment.

● Interest payments on the federal debt larger than the entire budget of 20 years ago.

● A federal budget out of balance by as much as $300 billion in 1985 and (according to J. Peter Grace, the head of the President's Private Sector Survey on Cost Control) by $616 billion a year in 1990 and $2.5 trillion a year by 2000, if current trends continue.

While Vietnam is the most spectacular, it is not the only example of elitist failure. The Vietnam War was conceived and directed by the establishment's best minds, from places like Harvard, Princeton, and Yale, but it was fought by boys from city slums and small towns. The elite proved to be bunglers who squandered 57,000 American lives and $80 billion while losing South Vietnam, Laos and Cambodia to communism. With wiser leadership, the war with its massive loss of life could have been avoided.

The foreign policy establishment, in fact, has a poor record in most parts of the world. For example, the establishment bet most of its chips on the Shah of Iran, praising him as a great leader and honoring him with a state dinner in Washington as late as 1977; then it turned on him. Refusing to permit him to enter the United States, the elite establishment caused him, in 1979 and 1980, to be shuttled from one country to another as he sought treatment for the cancer that was killing him. Even with the Shah's mistreatment at the hands of the Carter Administration, the elite failed to assuage the bitterness of his successors. One of the obvious results of that blunder is the fact that our Persian Gulf oil supplies are today in greater jeopardy than ever despite the expenditure of billions of tax dollars to protect them.

The elite failed to anticipate or respond adequately to the Soviet occupation of Afghanistan, from which the Soviets can threaten to interdict Persian Gulf oil shipments.

Red Chinese and Soviet influence, already dominant in many parts of Africa, is expanding at a rapid clip while U.S. influence wanes.

In Latin America, the establishment elite has deep sixed the Monroe Doctrine, but has failed to provide an alternative. The Soviet Union has expanded its power base from Cuba to Nicaragua. Central America is on the verge of a regional war. Mexico's ruling party is pro-Castro and its economy is in shambles. United States prestige, despite the Panama Canal giveaway which was hailed as a great soothing gesture, was at an all-time low until the invasion of Grenada.

The foreign policy blunders of the establishment might be forgiven if its mistakes had been accompanied by some clear measure of success in other areas.

But the establishment has blundered just as badly in domestic matters. In fiscal policy, the U.S. Government resembles a Third World nation, each year paying the interest on its massive debt and adding to the principal. The annual interest now equals the federal budget of 1960.

Establishment policies brought us double digit inflation that robbed the people of their savings and eroded their pension funds and insurance coverage. To stop the inflation, the Federal Reserve establishment pushed interest rates so high that the U.S. suffered its worst recession since the 1930's.

Establishment tax and trade policies neither protected American jobs nor greatly expanded American exports. If there is a rising tide of self-destructive protectionism in America, the elite has only itself to blame for promoting the politics of envy.

Establishment bankers have demonstrated once again that those who ignore history repeat history. Like the American banking establishment in the 1920s and its British counterpart in the 19th Century, the banking elite has overextended credit to foreign nations, some of which cannot now and perhaps never will be able to repay their loans. Despite their public confidence, the bankers live in dread of the inevitable—a default by one or more of the debtor nations.

Establishment educators and judicial activists have combined to destroy the effectiveness of the public schools so that today we spend more per pupil and get worse results than any other industrialized nation on earth.

The establishment's self-styled intellectuals, with their incessant attacks on traditional morality, have achieved what they wanted: a society free from Puritan hangups. But it is not the free, humane and healthy society they predicted. The Christian fundamentalists were correct in predicting that, with the abandonment of traditional morality, we would see an enormous rise in the rates of crime, suicide, venereal disease, teenage pregnancy, abortion, and illegitimacy. Frankly, I can't think of much that would shock most Americans today—and that shocks me.

Who is so bold as to oppose the establishment, to speak loudly and clearly against policies that have led to one failure after another? Certainly not the leaders of the two major political parties.

At present, elitists dominate both parties. Those in the GOP bail out the big banks that lend money to anti-American Third World and communist countries and provide tax credits and loan guarantees for doing business with foreign governments. Those in the Democratic party work to transfer economic power from productive citizens to bureaucrats by unnecessary regulation and overtaxation.

On most issues, there's not a dime's worth of difference between the elites of the two major parties. The elitist leaders of both parties support busing or accept it without much protest; they oppose school prayer, support high levels of spending on welfare programs, and oppose tax cuts. They want Congress to appropriate more money for the International Monetary Fund and for foreign aid, which bails out the big banks because the money in turn is used to pay the interest on loans from the Chase Manhattan Bank and other international banks. They oppose tuition tax credits and support trade with communist countries.

In the United States there has developed a broad elitist consensus on foreign policy, trade, most social issues, and economics. To be sure, this consensus is neither monolithic nor rigid. But roughly the same policies, with only minor variations in details and emphasis but sometimes with major variations in rhetoric, are carried over from one administration to the next regardless of which party occupies the White House.

It is not surprising to find Alexander Haig, nominee for secretary of state in a Republican administration, counseled at confirmation hearings by Joseph Califano, a cabinet officer in the previous Democratic administration. Nor is it surprising when, 18 months later, that process is repeated with Haig's successor, George Shultz, assisted by Lloyd Cutler, Jimmy Carter's White House counsel. There is a continuity of government that transcends the Republican and Democratic parties.

To a great degree, it doesn't matter who wins the presidential election: the establishment wins either way.

If one ignores rhetoric and judges an administration by what it does, it is clear that there is little difference between the Reagan foreign policy and the Carter foreign policy. In the heat of partisan debate, it is sometimes forgotten that after the Soviets invaded Afghanistan, Jimmy Carter assumed a much tougher stance and even ordered a sizeable increase in defense spending. It was Carter who imposed a grain embargo; it was Ronald Reagan who lifted it.

While the President makes speeches about the evils of communism, he bails out the Polish government and the banks to which it is indebted, agrees to an eventual cutoff of arms aid to Taiwan, and approves the sale of computers and other sophisticated gear to the Soviets. The sale of high technology gear to the Soviets is especially helpful to their military forces.

The President asks us to tighten our belts, but lobbies to increase by $8.4 billion the U.S. taxpayer's contribution to the International Monetary Fund, transferring that wealth from the American people to Third World countries and their creditors.

Ronald Reagan endorses Jimmy Carter's program of land confiscation in El Salvador and approves taxpayer funding for a loan to build a nuclear power plant in Soviet-controlled Rumania. He lifts sanctions against the Soviet pipeline and signs a five year sweetheart grain deal with the Soviets.

When the Soviets shoot down an unarmed commercial airliner with 269 persons on board, including Congressman Larry McDonald, President Reagan's response is so weak that it draws criticism from liberals such as Senator Paul Tsongas for not being forceful enough. Considering the weak sanctions imposed by the Administration, Tsongas charged that the Soviet Union was getting away "scot-free" with the attack. "The Soviets are not stupid," he said. "They understand the difference between real sanctions that hurt and things that in essence are public relations gimmicks."

On economic matters, the distinction between the parties is likewise blurred. For the most important economic position filled by the President, the chairmanship of the Federal Reserve Board, Reagan reappoints Carter's choice, Paul Volcker, a man whom millions of Americans rightly associate with tight money policies that either helped cause the 1981-82 recession or made it worse.

President Reagan increases federal funding for the National Endowments for the Arts and Humanities and the Corporation for Public Broadcasting, to provide entertainment for a mostly well-to-do audience that can afford to entertain itself. He increases taxes by $350 billion, hiring

5,200 additional IRS agents. He reverses much of the progress made during the Carter Administration toward deregulation of the trucking industry. By failing to veto unnecessary and counterproductive government spending, he helps produce the biggest budget deficits in history.

If this sounds like an attack on Ronald Reagan, it is not intended that way. He is simply carrying forward the policies set by his Democratic and Republican predecessors. The important point is that the two major political parties give the American people a choice between two competing elites, with a difference in rhetoric but little in substance. An echo, not a choice.

Both the Democratic and Republican parties call themselves the party of the people, but in fact neither party is correct in doing so. Each has come to defend a privileged elite against the will and interests of the majority. Both parties are led for the most part by members of the establishment who have more in common with each other than with the typical Democratic or Republican voter.

Who will speak for the little guy? The answer to that question will determine the direction of American politics during the remainder of this century.

In 1972, 1976, and 1980, the presidential election was won by the candidate who most appealed to the common man. In each campaign, the winning candidate was the one who spoke more convincingly of basic American values— the family, honesty, the work ethic, neighbor helping neighbor, fair pay for a day's labor, and peace through strength.

Nixon, Carter, and Reagan each campaigned against elitism but, once in office, each practiced it. Each president missed the opportunity he had to ensure long term majority status for his party by harnessing the most powerful force in contemporary American politics: the new populism.

Populism identifies with the "common man," that is, the man or woman who works for a living. It does not ridicule

America's Voice is a Populist Voice on Major Economic, Social and Defense Issues.

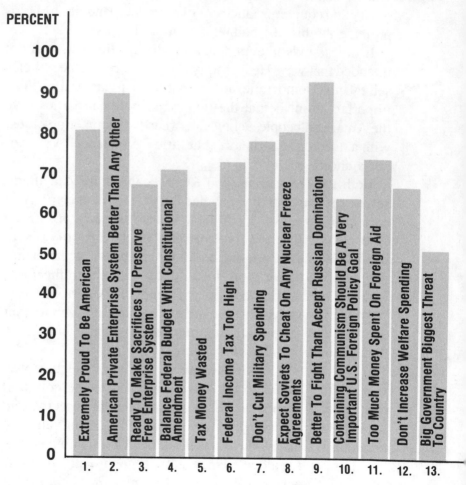

PERCENT

Bar chart with percent values. Bars labeled:

1. Extremely Proud To Be American
2. American Private Enterprise System Better Than Any Other
3. Ready To Make Sacrifices To Preserve Free Enterprise System
4. Balance Federal Budget With Constitutional Amendment
5. Tax Money Wasted
6. Federal Income Tax Too High
7. Don't Cut Military Spending
8. Expect Soviets To Cheat On Any Nuclear Freeze Agreements
9. Better To Fight Than Accept Russian Domination
10. Containing Communism Should Be A Very Important U.S. Foreign Policy Goal
11. Too Much Money Spent On Foreign Aid
12. Don't Increase Welfare Spending
13. Big Government Biggest Threat To Country

SOURCE

1. Civic Service, Inc. Poll, March 1981
2. Civic Service, Inc. Poll, March 1981
3. TIME/Yankelvich, Skelly & White Poll, June 1982
4. Gallup Poll, June 1983
5. ABC News/Washington Post Poll, August 1983
6. National Opinion Research Center, Spring 1982
7. Gallup Poll, January 1983
8. ABC News/Washington Post Poll, April 1982
9. Gallup Poll, February 1982
10. Gallup Poll, November 1982
11. Roper Poll, December 1982
12. Roper Poll, December 1982
13. Gallup Poll, May 1983
14. Harris & Associates, February 1981

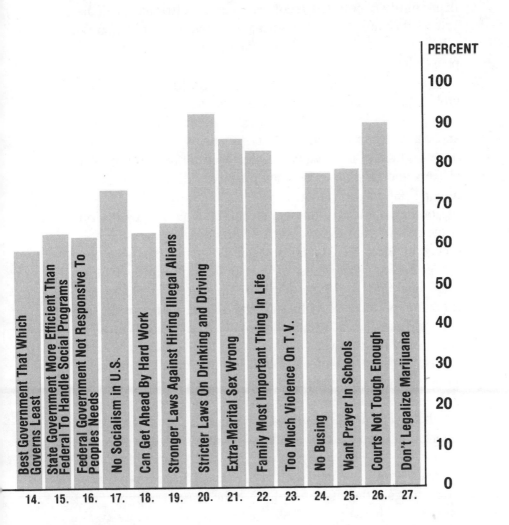

PERCENT

100
90
80
70
60
50
40
30
20
10
0

14. Best Government That Which Governs Least
15. State Government More Efficient Than Federal To Handle Social Programs
16. Federal Government Not Responsive To Peoples Needs
17. No Socialism in U.S.
18. Can Get Ahead By Hard Work
19. Stronger Laws Against Hiring Illegal Aliens
20. Stricter Laws On Drinking and Driving
21. Extra-Marital Sex Wrong
22. Family Most Important Thing In Life
23. Too Much Violence On T.V.
24. No Busing
25. Want Prayer In Schools
26. Courts Not Tough Enough
27. Don't Legalize Marijuana

14. 15. 16. 17. 18. 19. 20. 21. 22. 23. 24. 25. 26. 27.

15. Gallup Poll, October 1982
16. Roper Organization Poll, November 1981
17. Civic Service, Inc. Poll, March 1981
18. ABC News/Washington Post, August 1983
19. Gallup Poll, October 1982
20. Gallup Poll, March 1982
21. National Opinion Research Center, April 1982
22. Gallup Poll, January 1982
23. ABC News Poll, February 1983
24. CBS News/N.Y. Times Poll, March 1982
25. Gallup Poll, June 1982
26. National Opinion Research Center, April 1982
27. Gallup Poll, October 1982

his music, religion, or manner of dress. Thus, it is more than simply a political ideology; it is an attribute of character—it requires humility for a politician with control over other people's lives to admit that he is no better than the people he governs.

In a political sense, populism is not confined to the principles of the People's Party that had its greatest success during the 1890s. The populist movement of the late 19th and early 20th centuries was born out of the rage of the downtrodden at their victimization by establishment power brokers and creditors who used political influence to secure unfair financial advantages.

But the populists of that era promoted a quick fix solution to the problems of the average citizen: greater governmental power in their own hands instead of in the hands of the robber barons. After most of the populist platform was enacted into law, many members of the elite adapted to the changing political climate and maintained their power. In other cases, the old establishment was replaced by a new one just as oppressive.

I use the term, *populism,* to refer to the school of political thought that places emphasis on the rights of average citizens and defends those citizens against the concentration of political power in the hands of an elite. It stands for self-reliance, decentralization, and open and responsive government.

Populism represents the class of Americans variously referred to as "the little people," "the forgotten men and women," "the working class," and "the silent majority." It is distrustful of large institutions but fiercely patriotic.

It is a mistake to trace populism to the 1880s or 1890s. Founded on the individualist principles of the Declaration of Independence, it may be the oldest political tradition in America.

In 1824, Thomas Jefferson set forth the principle of populism when he defined the natural parties of mankind: "Men by their constitution are naturally divided into two parties. 1) Those who fear and distrust the people, and wish to draw all powers from them into the hands of the higher classes. 2) Those who identify themselves with the people, have confidence in them, cherish and consider them as the most honest and safe, although not the most wise depository of the public interests.

"In every country these two parties exist, and in every one where they are free to think, speak, and write, they will declare themselves. Call them, therefore, liberals and serviles, Jacobins and Ultras, Whigs and Tories, republicans and federalists, they are the same parties still and pursue the same object."

Or call them, as I do, elitists and populists.

For decades, the party of the aristocratic establishment has been in charge of the U.S. government. Repeatedly the people have placed their hopes on politicians whose candidacies have been based on populist themes, but whose terms in office have been noted for preservation of the power of the establishment.

Today, the middle class is eager for dramatic change. The working people of America want a champion who will stand up for them against those who abuse their power. The question is: Who will lead the new populist movement?

To answer that question, we must first take an in-depth look at the forces that will stand in the way of such a movement—Big Business, Big Labor, and Big Government, and their allies in the fields of international finance, education, the law, and the media.

2 / Big Government

The American system is unique in all the world and in all history. Never before had a government been founded on the basis of a voluntary association of free individuals. Never before had a government expressly limited its own powers, in order to promote liberty and diversity among its own people.

In the two centuries since the founding of the Republic, a few nations have imitated the American system, but none has duplicated its success and longevity.

Today we face a serious challenge to the American system. The government has grown so large that it no longer responds adequately to democratic control. It has taken on a life of its own, independent of the people's will.

Anyone from the real world who visits Washington and pays attention to the public discussion of issues is astounded at the attitude of the city toward the rest of America. Unfortunately, our nation's capital does not have a monopoly on condescension toward the average citizen; many people in government consciously or unconsciously share that view.

That attitude is obvious in the way government goes about helping people. Federal spending on income transfer and welfare programs is eight times the amount needed to raise every person in America above the poverty line, yet the government tells us that 32 million people live below that line. Why is so much spent with so little to show for it? One reason is that the money is divided among hundreds of different programs, each with its own rules of eligibility.

The unspoken assumption of the welfare bureaucracy is that poor people just don't have enough sense to use money for food unless it comes to them in the form of food stamps; that they aren't smart enough to use money to pay their rent unless it is given to them in the form of housing subsidies; and so forth.

It is not just the poor whom the government assumes to be stupid. How many government regulations exist to prevent us from doing harm to ourselves? Herbert Spencer had the perfect response to government paternalism: "To protect men from their own folly is to people the world with fools."

With government regulation of everything from milk prices to whether automobiles must have airbags, the question must be asked: Who's in charge here? Do we run the government, or does the government run us?

As Milton Friedman points out, you can't work as a lawyer, a doctor, a dentist, a plumber, a barber, or an undertaker without first getting a license from the government. You can't start a bank or a taxicab service, sell electricity or groceries, run a railroad or a busline without first getting permission from the government.

A good example of how government at even the lowest level can work against the best interests of the people is the taxicab business in New York City and Washington, D.C.

In New York, one must have a "medallion" to operate a taxicab. The present cost of a medallion to an independent taxi owner-operator is about $70,000. As a result, thousands of gypsy or illegal taxicabs have sprung up because of the failure of the medallion taxis to provide adequate service. Meanwhile, the number of medallion cabs has remained the same for decades because of the high cost of medallions.

In contrast, in Washington, D.C., which permits open entry into the taxicab industry, the law of supply and demand has produced almost 9,000 taxis (compared with about 12,000 legal taxis in New York City, which has 10 times the population of Washington, D.C.).

As economist Walter Williams states, open entry for taxis in Washington has produced "business ownership or work opportunities for many semi-skilled workers, college students and others" and provided "higher quality service at a lower price."

Walter Williams, by the way, is one of America's most remarkable economists; not simply for his ability to expose liberal, elitist economic fallacies, but for his ability to withstand the criticism and worse of his peers. Williams is black, and black leaders like Jesse Jackson, Benjamin Hooks and others are very critical when economists point out that welfare has hurt, not helped, black Americans.

But that is the truth. After more than 20 years of public housing, food stamps, day care centers, minimum wage increases, and all the other Great Society nostrums, black America is in far worse shape today than before. More than half of America's black children do not have a father in the home. Crime, alcoholism, and drug abuse continue to escalate in the inner cities.

Welfare programs are defended as essential to securing jobs for poor blacks, but what they really do is provide employment for middle class, usually white, bureaucrats. In fact, as George Gilder points out, "the War on Poverty managed to triple black unemployment during the very decade of the 1970's when a higher proportion of Americans got jobs than ever before in peacetime."

It is mostly through well meaning but ill-advised programs that the government became the bloated, extravagant, inefficient monster it is today.

It took the government 175 years for its annual budget to reach $100 billion, in 1962. It then took only nine years for the budget to top $200 billion.

Four years later, in 1975, it hit $300 billion and two years later $400 billion. In 1980, it went over $600 billion, and President Reagan's budget for 1984 will be close to $900 billion.

The government now consumes about one quarter of the Gross National Product (which itself includes government spending). With state and local taxation figured in, the government's share approaches 40 percent.

Many of us hoped and believed that under the Reagan Administration, federal spending would decrease, but it has increased in the domestic area. Housing aid is up 75 percent under Reagan, food stamps up 32 percent, Medicare up 63 percent, Social Security up 44 percent.

During the first three years of the Reagan Administration, state and local spending increased 27 percent, but federal spending ballooned 41 percent. And Ronald Reagan is supposed to be a conservative President!

Why is even a Ronald Reagan, who complained about Big Government for nearly 30 years before his election, unable to do anything about the size of government? Because the special interests that feed off the taxpayer have had years to build a well oiled public relations machine, to install like-minded individuals in important positions in the news media and on Congressional staffs. They have been assisted in that effort by the ever-growing federal bureaucracy, which has actively contributed to the development of anti-taxpayer organizations.

For example, according to the April 1982 *Conservative Digest*, the U.S. government paid Tom Hayden, Jane Fonda's husband and a founder of the radical Students for a Democratic Society, $189,000 to train VISTA volunteers. The Feminist Press got $313,000 from the Department of

Education in two grants "for the improvement of postsecondary education." The National Welfare Rights Organization got the services of 71 VISTA-funded volunteers.

Other examples of your tax dollars at work include:

● A CETA grant that provided $640,000 for the Seattle Gay Youth Theater Project.

● A Department of Education grant that provided $275,000 to the National Organization for Women Legal Defense and Education Fund.

● $148,000 spent by the federally-funded Corporation for Public Broadcasting to publicize Solidarity Day, the massive Washington protest against tax and spending cuts.

● Nine grants totalling $611,000 to the Sierra Club, a blatantly political group that worked unceasingly for the resignation of Interior Secretary James Watt.

● The use of 11 VISTA volunteers by the Institute for the Study of Human Values to prepare the publications "The Reagan Cruelty Index" and "The Greed Index—A Guide to the Reagan Tax Cuts."

● $41,000 for "The Leaping Lesbian Follies," a show performed in the nude.

The amount of each such grant is small. But added together, federal grants provide literally billions of taxpayers dollars each year for thousands of left-wing organizations.

The federal government has nurtured a community of people which makes its living not by honest work, but by handouts from politicians. Government programs channel hundreds of billions of dollars through administrators, statisticians, economists, sociologists, think tanks, social agencies, universities, and bureaucrats. Monstrous boondoggles are justified on the ground that, if only enough money is spent on a program, some benefit will trickle down to the people the programs are meant to serve.

The special interests who are the real beneficiaries of these programs care little about expanded growth and economic opportunity. They see life as a zero sum game, where one side wins only if the other loses, and they believe that it is the job of the government to decide who wins and who loses.

They believe that there is a limit to the amount of wealth that society can produce, and that we have reached that limit. In their view, which runs counter to the whole of human history, there are only so many products that can be made, so many factories that can be built, and so many jobs that can be created. Their concern is how to divide society's wealth, not how to produce more for everyone.

Their philosophy divides America into competing interest groups, with each group fighting for its share of a stagnant economy. They would pit old against young (for example, the Social Security bailout), North against South (proposals to prohibit companies from moving factories without government permission), and black against white (racial quotas). They care less about increasing the standard of living of society as a whole than about ensuring that misery is fairly distributed.

Congressman Newt Gingrich (R-Ga.) explains it this way: "The welfare state sees everyone as a victim. If you're a dairy farmer and you produce too much milk and butter, the welfare state will help you by stepping in through the government and reducing the amount of milk and butter produced, in order to raise the price.

"That means that, if you're a housewife, you're a victim because now when you go to shop you won't be able to afford the milk and butter, so the welfare state will give you food stamps.

"That means that, if you're a textile worker, when you

go and get your paycheck, you won't have enough money because the government just took it all out for the dairy farmer and the housewife, so the welfare state will give you a subsidized loan. And on and on. . . .''

The elitists in Washington believe that a fair distribution of the nation's wealth can be brought about only if it is controlled by the government, that is, by the elitists in Washington. They want the government's share of the nation's wealth to be larger next year than it was last year, and larger in each succeeding year. They want people to have less money in their pockets so that they will be more dependent on government. They want government to have more money so that the politicians who support the bureaucracy can buy the votes necessary to remain in office.

Politicians trade among themselves, a bridge in this district for a dam in this, in a sort of *Monopoly* game in which the bank (the taxpayers) always lends out enough money to keep the players from going bankrupt. Much of the waste in government can be traced to the Washington buddy system of members of Congress, the bureaucracy, and special interest groups who promote programs they want, but the nation doesn't need.

Consider the Clinch River breeder reactor, a $3-8 billion boondoggle that private companies won't touch without a 100 percent government guarantee on their investment. Senator Gordon Humphrey says: "Conservatives have been under the impression that a vote against Clinch River is a vote against nuclear power, and that is just not so. The truth is that Clinch River is a nothing but a plutonium porkbarrel.''

The cost overrun on Clinch River has been estimated at between 900 and 1,850 percent since 1977. If the project ever gets on line, the energy produced will cost the equivalent of $76 to $149 per barrel of oil.

The Clinch River project, which at this writing is still hanging on despite efforts to kill it, is very important to

Senate Majority Leader Howard Baker (R-TN). One reason that cost conscious members of Congress have been unable to end funding of the project is because that Western Senators who want water projects in their home states want to keep the majority leader happy, so the taxpayers end up paying for Clinch River *and* the water projects.

Then there's the Garrison Diversion Unit, costing $1.3 billion, which Senators Mark Andrews (R.) and Quentin Burdick (D.) of North Dakota are pushing. It would irrigate about 250,000 acres of farmland while flooding 220,000 acres. Its 3,000-mile system of canals, reservoirs, pipelines and drains would benefit fewer than 1,000 farms. It would destroy or degrade at least 12 national wildlife refuges. Is this in the public interest? No, but since when did the public interest matter when there's pork to be had?

The workings of the Washington buddy system were especially obvious when the Tennessee-Tombigbee Waterway, in effect an effort to build a second Mississippi River, narrowly survived a challenge in 1982. Senator Howell Heflin (D-Ala.) pleaded with his colleagues to continue the $3 billion project because Senator John Stennis (D- Miss.) could not be reelected without it. Congressman Tom Bevill (D-Ala.), Chairman of the House Appropriations Committee Subcommittee on Energy and Water Projects, reportedly made it clear to his colleagues that their votes on Tenn-Tom would determine the fate of their own projects (Bevill denies that he made any threats).

Senator Charles Percy (R-Ill.) proposed making Alabama and Mississippi pay half the cost of completing the project, but Percy backed off—reportedly in fear that the same requirement for a local contribution would be imposed on a lock and dam at Alton, Illinois. Percy aide Hal Smith said, "People who had an interest in Tenn-Tom did call us and say, 'You're going to lose some southern votes on Lock and Dam 26 if you're not careful.'"

From Senator Orrin Hatch's (R-Utah) efforts on the $1.5 billion Central Utah project, to Senator John Glenn's (D-Ohio) work on the $8-10 billion Gas Centrifuge Enrichment Plant near Portsmouth, Ohio, to Senator Robert Byrd's (D-W.Va.) rescue of the wasteful Amtrak Cardinal line, the Washington buddy system wastes the hard earned money of America's working people. For Congressmen, "You vote for my project and I'll vote for yours" are words to live by.

The most unfortunate result of Congress playing with other people's money is its effect on the national defense. When the House Armed Services Committee cut the defense budget for Fiscal Year 1983, it added $296 million for military construction projects *not* requested by the Pentagon. Districts represented by the Military Installations and Facilities Subcommittee, 3.2 percent of the House, got 58 percent of the add-ons, according to *Congressional Quarterly*.

The Senate Armed Services Committee did not do likewise for the 1983 budget. But in the 1982 budget it added $152 million in funding for non-requested projects; 88 percent of that money went for projects in the home states of members of the committee.

Given the grand history of Congress, it is depressing to look upon its members today who often seem to be more interested in feathering their own nests than in caring for the general welfare of the nation.

To begin with, they are certainly well paid at $69,000 a year. They have liberal retirement benefits with pensions often higher than the salaries they received as Members of Congress.

They have rent-free offices in Washington and as many as three at home. They have free mailing privileges for "office business" mail, plus allowances for airmail and special delivery.

THE SKYROCKETING COST OF RUNNING CONGRESS 1960-1982

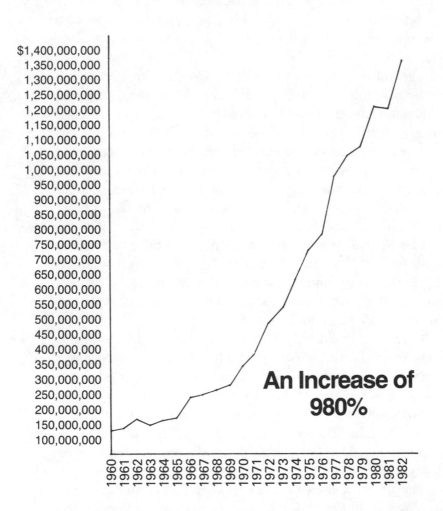

They have hundreds of hours of free long distance telephone calls, a generous telegram allowance, a handsome
stationery allowance, and free round trips home—18 a year
for House members, more for a Senator.

They have free parking, free emergency medical care,
free drugs if prescribed by Capitol physicians, a government-
subsidized health plan, free swimming pools and gyms, free
flowers for offices and entertaining, free picture framing,
subsidized meals at private dining rooms in the Capitol, and
discount rates on TV and radio studio services.

They are exempt from jury duty, the Freedom of Information Act, OSHA, the Civil Rights Act of 1964, the Equal
Employment Opportunity Act, the Fair Labor Standards Act,
the National Labor Relations Act, and the Age Discrimination in Employment Act.

Many work only three days a week in Washington. They
are members of the infamous "Tuesday to Thursday Club",
flying into the capital on Monday and flying out on Friday.

That many within the Congress have profited by that
charity-begins-at-home theory cannot be denied. Many of
them who constantly complain that they are underpaid, are
in fact a privileged class exempt from many of the cares
and worries of common people. Along with bureaucrats,
White House aides, and Presidents, they have taken advantage of us for too long, and have too long taken us for
granted.

They have nearly bankrupted our country and our children
with their reckless spending for social ends which you and
I neither share nor want.

The waste must stop. The abuses must be ended. Congress
and the Executive Branch must become responsible and
responsive to us and to common sense.

We simply cannot afford to go on spending as we have.
The day of reckoning is near at hand, but it is not yet too
late. We can and must take steps to get out-of-control spend-

ing under control and to make government at all levels, federal, state and local—our servant, not our master.

The principal idea behind the growth of the Washington establishment is that a bureaucrat sitting in an office on the Potomac knows better than you how to live your life. How absurd!

Yet, even such a ridiculous proposition is taken seriously by most politicians. As this is written, Democratic presidential candidates are falling over each other to come up with an "industrial policy," a centralized plan for the economy which eliminates economic freedom in manufacturing. Industrial policy may be a major issue of the 1984 campaign, despite the fact that centralized planning has been an abject failure throughout human history.

There is a good reason for this. As the great economist Ludwig von Mises has pointed out, no individual or group managing a central economic plan can respond quickly to changes in circumstances, compared to millions of individuals in a free economy. "The alternative," he says, "is not plan or no plan. The question is: Whose planning? Should each member of society plan for himself or should the paternal government plan for all? The issue is . . . freedom versus government omnipotence."

Dr. Paul McCracken, former Chairman of the President's Council of Economic Advisors, offered a parable: Imagine some space travelers, dispatched to earth to determine which countries had planned economies and which had unplanned economies.

After six months, the aliens issue a report listing the planned economies, including the U.S., Japan, West Germany, and Hong Kong. The report also lists the unplanned economies, including the USSR, Red China, East Germany, and North Korea.

A government official tells the aliens that they have it exactly reversed. The aliens correct him by pointing out that, in the economies like the U.S., there are autos in the showrooms, clothes on the racks, and food on the shelves in the stores. In the economies patterned on the USSR, there are long lines for food and clothing, and only the relatively wealthy can afford automobiles (for which the wait is measured in years). Surely the U.S.-type economies are the planned ones!

Dr. McCracken's story illustrates an important lesson: that the only kind of "economic plan" that works is one that allows the economy to operate free of government meddling.

During the lifetime of my 79-year-old father we have progressed from the Wright Brothers at Kitty Hawk to six-year-olds programming computers at home. Imagine for a moment what our country would be like if politicians and bureaucrats had controlled our lives during that time. We might have buggy whips piling up in government warehouses as part of an effort to protect the jobs of buggy-whip makers.

The elitists respond to this argument by claiming that the U.S. government, armed with the greatest information-gathering apparatus in the world, is able to project our future needs much better than the free market. But the fact is that the government has no idea what economic conditions will be like in the nation as a whole three months from now, much less in specific industries a decade in the future.

In *Inquiry* magazine, economist Thomas Hazlett writes that the Office of Management and Budget's estimates of the federal deficit have been within 25 percent of the actual figure only three times in the last 14 years. Four times it overestimated by between 44 percent and 141 percent. Hazlett says the 1974-75 recession was "wholly overlooked by 31 of the 32 major . . . models" for forecasting the future of the economy.

In 1982, The *Washington Post* reported that "the consensus forecast at the start of a quarter has been wrong five out of the last seven times about whether GNP would go up or down during the following three months.'' In terms of probability, you would do better three times out of four to flip a coin than to rely on the consensus of our economic experts.

If the world's brightest economists in and out of government are unable to predict the future direction of the economy, how can the government decide which industries should be subsidized and which should be taxed out of existence as part of an industrial policy? Again, the alternative is not *plan* or *no plan*; the question is *whose plan*?

The attitude that ''Washington knows best'' extends beyond economic matters. One widely quoted definition of politics is *the authoritative allocation of values*, that is, the imposition of certain values upon society by government. Those values may be well intentioned (racial equality, consumer safety, a clean environment) or blatantly abusive (minimum prices, ''value-free'' sex education, bans on multi-family housing). The theme running throughout the last few decades has been that of Washington's values imposed on the rest of America, instead of the other way around.

One indication of the growth of the power of Washington in our lives is *U.S. News and World Report*'s annual survey of the most influential persons in America. Each year, *U.S. News* surveys leaders in 30 fields to determine who exercises ''the most influence in national life—whether through position, ability, personality, or wealth.''

As analyzed by Howard Means in an article in *The Washingtonian* magazine, ''For Better or Worse We Now Run America,'' the 1982 list of the most influential leaders in America was ''a reflection of changes in the relation of America to its capital . . . a record of eighteen months of failure on the side of Ronald Reagan's forces to [decentralize] the national government.''

Means took the list of the 20 most influential leaders and

assigned 20 points for first place, 19 points for second, etc. Based on his analysis, updated with the results of the 1983 survey, we find that representatives of the public sector were more than five times as powerful as representatives of the private sector. Within government, non-elected officials were 43 percent more powerful than elected ones.

In the 1983 survey, ten of the top twenty were born in the East, including four in New York City. Thirteen of the twenty had degrees from Ivy League schools. Of the 14 who held elective or appointive office, only five had significant experience outside of public life. Not one person from outside of Washington made the top ten in either 1982 or 1983.

As Means concluded, "It is customary to say that Washington's influence is on the wane, that power is falling to the cities and states, that power is spreading itself broadly across America as the population disperses out of the Northeast into the Sun Belt states and the West. But in a technocracy, enduring power will always fall into the hands of the technocrats, to the fine-tuners and manipulators, to the political operatives who can grease the increasingly complex channels of decision-making."

The *U.S. News* survey is just one indication of the growing influence of a Washington that has already grown beyond anything that even the New Dealers could have imagined. The very size of the public sector in the capital city distorts its view of the rest of America and the rest of the world. Reading *The Washington Post* every day can give you the idea that 95 percent of everything important happens inside the Beltway (the highway that surrounds the city).

Hugh Sidey of *Time* magazine calls it "a classic perversity of Washington. The dialogue and mood of the capital are often controlled by the 50,000 men and women who work as lobbyists, legislative aides and journalists. They are nurtured, entertained, and often guided by trivial events and gossip. Many of the 15,000 lobbyists get paid on the basis of their access to the White House staff and congressional leaders. . . . The Congress is now freighted with 20,000 employees, many of whom spend their time plotting how to help or thwart the Administration. The 15,000 Washington journalists feed off these 35,000 sources and frequently mistake their priorities for those of the country at large.''

Following the dictates of the privileged class of lobbyists, legislative aides, journalists, our government has expanded its scope far beyond anything envisioned in the wildest nightmares of the Founding Fathers. The federal system has become, in Jefferson's phrase, ''a government of wolves over sheep.''

Attempts to restrain government are reported by the media as attacks on poor people, or on minorities, or on some other group of ''victims.'' Senator Jeremiah Denton (R-Ala.) has pointed out, ''When responsible lawmakers try to reduce the size of the federal government, the groups that feed off it organize marches and mobilize their public relations departments to attack that effort. They shout that we are trying to hurt the needy.

''By 'the needy,' they mean themselves.''

The reaction of the special interest groups is predictable. In 1975, Ronald Reagan was asked what would happen if anyone tried to take power away from the government establishment and give it back to the people. His 1975 response: ''There will be howls of protest from every carpeted anteroom and chauffered limousine in Washington. But we must turn a deaf ear to them if our nation is to survive.'' Reagan was exactly right.

3 / Big Business

Many of our political leaders and big businessmen use the term "capitalism" to describe the use of governmental power to benefit business, especially big business. Their understanding of capitalism is summed up in the statement of a corporate executive, "What's good for General Motors is good for the country."

The so-called capitalism supported by the corporate and political elite entails government subsidies, minimum and maximum prices, tax loopholes for politically-favored activities, and preservation of the status quo (which, as Ronald Reagan used to say, is Latin for "the mess we're in").

But the system the establishment supports is not really capitalism. True capitalism is an economic system free of governmental interference, in which all businesses, big and small, are free to succeed—or to fail.

In opposition to a system of government assistance to business, Adam Smith wrote the first great book of economics, *The Wealth of Nations* (1776). Dugald Stewart summarized Smith's argument: "The most effective plan for advancing a people . . . is by allowing every man, as long as he observes the rules of justice, to pursue his own interest in his own way, and to bring forth his industry and his capital into the freest competition with those of his fellow citizens. Every system of policy which endeavors . . . to draw towards a particular species of industry a greater share of the capital of the society than would naturally go to it . . . is, in reality, subversive of the great purpose which it means to promote.''

In general, the Founding Fathers were very much in accord with Smith's reasoning. Thomas Jefferson even proposed a constitutional amendment to prohibit Congress from denying anyone the right to compete with an existing business.

During the 1800s, farmers and workers were exploited by large corporations that had access to political power and used it to create monopolies. For example, the Central Pacific Railroad used bribery to gain control of the California legislature, which cut off access by other railroad companies to California ports for three decades. The CP's rates were so high that it was more expensive to ship a keg of nails from New York to California overland by rail than around the tip of South America.

Between 1863 and 1867, some 100 million acres of land were given to the railroads to subsidize the construction of tracks across the continent. The fortunate railroads that received the grants received monopolies on each line, and the grants enabled them to overcome the natural advantages held by other methods of transportation west, such as boats and horsedrawn wagons.

The success of these railroads resulted not from good judgment, hard work, or even luck, but from political connections. The rich got richer and the poor got poorer—not due to any defect in the capitalist system, but because the rich had money with which to bribe legislators.

In his book *The Triumph of Conservatism*, Gabriel Kolko wrote, ''The dominant fact of American political life at the beginning of this century was that big business led the struggle for regulation of the economy. . . . Nor was it possible for many businessmen to ignore the fact that, in addition to sanctions the federal government might provide to ward off hostile criticisms, the national government was still an attractive potential source of windfall profits, subsidies, and resources.''

The 19th Century populists wanted to break up the great concentration of wealth that had resulted from abuse of the political process, but they were not anti-business. At the Democratic Convention of 1896, William Jennings Bryan electrified his audience when he referred to a remark by an earlier speaker and said:

''You have made the definition of a business man too limited in its application. The man who is employed for wages is as much a business man as his employer. The attorney in a country town is as much a business man as the corporation counsel in a great metropolis. The merchant at the cross-roads store is as much a business man as the merchant of New York. The farmer who goes forth in the morning and toils all day . . . is as much a business man as the man who goes on the board of trade and bets upon the price of grain. The miners who go down a thousand feet into the earth . . . are as much business men as the few financial magnates who, in a back room, corner the money of the world. We come to speak for this broader class of business man.''

The 19th Century populists intended to distribute power fairly throughout society, using the government as a means toward that end. Unfortunately, they failed to distinguish between those who became wealthy by the sweat of their brow and those who used the power of government to lift money from the purses of their fellow citizens.

That error would be fatal to their cause, though few realized it at the time. As the planks of the populist platform were adopted by the major parties and enacted into law, the workers and farmers of the populist movement discovered, too late, that they had failed to break up the great concentrations of power. For the most part, they hadn't even substituted a new elite for the old one. What they had done was to make it possible for the old elite to maintain power through the control of an increasingly centralized government.

Some of the most famous establishment figures of modern times, including Rockefeller, Ford, and Carnegie, came from the lower classes. Once at the top, many great businessmen of humble origins realized that they could never rest or be free from the incessant competition from below. They and their heirs began to use political influence to ensure their freedom from competition.

After climbing the ladder of free enterprise to success, they decided to pull it up after them. As part of the establishment, they came to fear the tendency of capitalism to raise people from the lower economic classes to positions of wealth and power. They favored a system of government monopolies that would prevent the untimely rise of the "little guy."

For many years, the railroads tried unsuccessfully to fix prices, but invariably one or more of the partners to the scheme would violate the agreement and it would collapse. It became clear that only the government had the power to enforce price-fixing agreements, so the Interstate Commerce Commission was created in 1887. Its purpose was to ensure that consumers would not receive the benefits of free competition.

For example, many carriers offered lower rates on long hauls, both because of economies of scale and because the greater the distance between two points, the greater the number of possible routes and the greater the competition. Sometimes these discounts resulted in a higher charge for a haul between two points on a given route than a haul between the two ends of the route. The ICC's solutions to this "problem" (which, of course, was no problem at all to the person receiving the benefit of the lower-than-usual rate) was to *increase* rates on the long hauls.

Richard Olney, U.S. Attorney General under President Cleveland, put it this way: The ICC "satisfies the popular clamor for a Government supervision of railroads, at the same time that that supervision is almost entirely nominal. Further, the older such a commission gets to be, the more inclined it will be found to take the business and railroad view of things. It thus becomes a sort of barrier between the railroad corporations and the people and a sort of protection against hasty and crude legislation hostile to railroad interests."

At first the ICC restricted only the railroads. But a new industry, interstate trucking, began to cut into the railroads' profits by depriving them of their virtual monopoly over land transportation of goods. New businesses were being created, new fortunes were being made, and manufacturers and merchants no longer had to pay the prices demanded by the railroads.

To combat this menace to the railroads' profits, interstate trucking was brought under ICC control by the Motor Carrier Act of 1935.

By restricting entry into the trucking business, initially to protect the railroads, the ICC protected those already in the trucking business. What began as a government agency to protect the railroads from free enterprise turned much of its attention to protecting the trucking industry from free enterprise.

For many years, you could engage in interstate trucking only after you got a certificate of authority from the ICC. You could obtain that certificate by convincing the ICC that your entry into the trucking business would not compete with someone already working the route you wanted to serve, or you could buy a certificate from a current holder.

If you tried to convince the ICC to grant you a new certificate, the process took years and might have cost you hundreds of thousands of dollars in legal fees as you sought to prove that your services are "needed." If you tried to buy a certificate from a current holder, it likewise cost you dearly. (For example, shortly before recent moves toward deregulation, the cost of a national operating permit for a moving company was estimated at $15 million.)

After the trucking industry was partially deregulated, beginning in 1980, the result was exactly as would be expected. The industry's representatives, management and labor alike, rushed to Congress to complain that the ICC was making it too easy to enter the trucking business.

Throughout the government, when private enterprise comes under government regulation, the pattern is repeated. An agency is created to protect the so-called public interest. Then it imposes restrictions that have the effect of restricting entry into an industry, thereby protecting existing businesses and unions from competition and from the resulting pressure to provide better service at lower prices.

Only rarely does government reduce its regulation of an industry. When it does, the consumer almost always benefits.

In 1980, Congress began to deregulate the airline industry. By the summer of 1983, most major airlines which practiced sound management and marketing were doing well. Other less efficient airlines were in serious trouble, as they should have been. More Americans were flying than ever before, 85 to 90 percent of them on the basis of special reduced fares.

New companies, not just commuter or feeder lines but intercontinental lines as well, appeared virtually overnight, serving consumers at rates unheard of in recent times. For example, the standard operating procedure followed when People's Express entered a new market was to offer service at 70 percent of the established price.

Of course, airline unions have joined with the management of the less efficient airlines to demand *re*regulation of the industry. But at this writing it appears that the hard-won gains of 1980-83, toward free enterprise in the airline industry, will be preserved.

Until 1980, government regulation became more and more oppressive each year. There is still much to be done.

It doesn't matter whether the competition, or potential competition, comes from another state or another country. With its great influence in the halls of power, big business will find some way to get a subsidy, an exclusive franchise, or an import restriction to "protect" consumers from the benefits of free enterprise.

If Joe's Auto Dealership charges more for its cars than the public wishes to pay, it goes out of business. If Chrysler does the same thing, the taxpayer is obliged to guarantee a $1.5 billion loan until it "gets back on its feet," that is, until economic conditions enable the public to pay higher prices for Chrysler's products.

Most government activities that benefit politically-connected businesses are far more subtle than bailouts like Chrysler's. The federal government spends some $6.3 billion a year on the administration of 57 regulatory agencies, plus tens of billions more to support the prices of various goods, but that figure is peanuts compared to what unnecessary regulation, government price supports, and import controls cost the consumer.

For example, the Interstate Commerce Commission spends about $56 million each year regulating transportation—but the monopolies it creates cost us an additional $10 *billion*. That $10 billion amount does not show up on any ledger and isn't counted when the government estimates its spending.

In almost every area of business the government prohibits

competition from persons offering products of higher quality or at lower prices, thus creating literal or shared monopolies.

A minimum wage law, with no exception for youth, protects labor unions from competition and keeps young people, especially young minorities, out of the workforce. Persons without work experience cannot get experience by selling their labor at a rate below the minimum wage.

In many industries, foreign countries are limited in the amount of goods that can be sold in the U.S. These laws protect domestic industries and unions from competition by allowing them to charge consumers higher prices (which, of course, means that consumers have less money to spend on other things). Old-time populists recognized protectionism as a method of ripping off the average working person to benefit the business establishment, and modern populists must recognize that as well.

In an effort to keep the price of agricultural products artificially high, the government strictly controls the amount of production or promises to buy, at a predetermined price, all that can be produced. "Marketing orders" allow growers of lemons, walnuts, navel and valencia oranges, and various other agricultural commodities to decide who can grow the crops, how much they can ship, and when. Each year, the government spends $2.5 billion to purchase dairy products (plus $60 million to store the surplus of milk, butter, and cheese that inevitably accumulates) in order to increase the price of dairy products by some $1.2 billion a year.

In addition to indirect subsidies such as grants of monopoly and minimum prices, the federal government provides many direct subsidies as well.

● The Synthetic Fuels Corporation and the Energy Information Administration subsidize research and development projects that the energy companies can and should pay for themselves. The fossil energy R&D program alone has an estimated cost of $428 million for fiscal 1984.

● The Maritime Administration provides annual subsidies of $150 million for construction of U.S. flagships and $300 million for their operation.

● The National Forest system loses $200 million a year by selling timber at below-market prices.

● The Export-Import Bank subsidizes foreigners' purchase of Americans goods at a cost of nearly $4 billion a year. Seven large companies receive two-thirds of that subsidy.

How do they get away with it? It's simple. The establishment discourages dissent by making its opinions the only socially acceptable ones. Thus, it is often able to overrule the dictates of common sense.

Common sense tells us that we cannot profit by giving money to people to buy things from us (as the Export-Import Bank does). Common sense tells us that you cannot fill people's empty bellies by slaughtering six million pigs and plowing under 11 million acres of cotton to manipulate agricultural prices (as the Agricultural Adjustment Administration did in the 1930s, at the depth of the Depression).

Unfortunately, a government run by the establishment elite is not directed by the common sense of the common people.

I have detailed ways in which big business uses the power of government to eliminate the threat of competition. Of course, most of that activity is perfectly legal, since it is done through the legislative process. But just because something is *legal* doesn't make it *right*.

The responsibility of business is to make as much money as it can in an honorable, legal way, by providing consumers with the goods and services they want. But as millions of small businessmen in the Jaycees and similar organizations have recognized, business people have a moral duty to work for the improvement of society as a whole. It is not a duty that can or should be imposed by government, because it is the same duty that all citizens have toward others.

Certainly business people have a responsibility not to take actions that will harm society by contributing to the breakdown of traditional morality. In that regard, many persons in big business have failed miserably.

A "buzzard advertiser" is a sponsor who picks up a television program after other sponsors have withdrawn. Often this occurs as a result of the program's offensive content. The National Federation for Decency has named Alberto-Culver as one such advertiser. Among programs that have carried Alberto-Culver's ads, according to NFD, are "Flesh and Blood," "The Users," "The Women's Room," "Scruples," "Anatomy of a Seduction," "Gay Power/Gay Politics," and "Amateur Night at the Dixie Bar and Grill."

NFD keeps a list of the companies that sponsor television's most offensive programming. Topping that list, in order, are RCA, Mazda, Tampax, I.C. Industries (including Dad's Root Beer and Midas), Helene Curtis, Beecham, Pabst, Denny's, Esmark (including Peter Pan Peanut Butter, Playtex, and Butterball Turkeys), and Warner Lambert (including Bromo-Seltzer, Listerine, and Dentyne).

RCA is #2 on *Fortune* magazine's list of diversified service companies. In the Fortune 500, I.C. Industries is #94, Pabst is #389, and Warner Lambert is #119.

And then there are companies whose advertising itself is offensive. There is the Calvin Klein jeans ad in which teenage actress Brooke Shields smiles coyly at the camera and says, "You know what comes between me and my Calvins? Nothing." The camera lingers on Miss Shields' taut jeans.

There is the radio ad for American Home Products' Semicid, the "vaginal insert that's easy to use . . . isn't messy or awkward or inconvenient." In its print ads, the company states that Semicid "doesn't affect your spontaneity or offend your senses. It has no unpleasant odor or taste.''

One wishes the same could be said of Semicid's advertising campaign.

The big business elite takes advantage of the little guy in another indirect way as well. It has been estimated that, each year, Americans must spend some $60-80 billion on national defense programs made necessary by corporations that do business with the Soviets. I am referring to the sale of equipment that is used to build Soviet weapons, and to the transfer of high technology that occurs when American companies trade with the Soviet Union.

Indeed, some corporations sell equipment to the Soviet Union, then turn around and sell equipment to the U.S. Department of Defense. Often the U.S. needs the equipment only because of the earlier sale to the Soviets. There is a term for corporations that work both sides of the street: *war profiteers*.

Most of this trade is perfectly legal. But I believe that business people have a responsibility to their country not to participate in activities that support our enemies. That responsibility transcends the question of whether what they do is technically legal or illegal.

The sales to the Soviet Union with the greatest long-term impact on the balance of power have been those involving high-technology products such as computers. The sellers have included such blue chip industrial giants as IBM, Control Data, Sperry-Rand, and General Electric.

Computers are essential to modern warfare. They are used for navigation and for weapons guidance in missiles, aircraft, tanks, satellite surveillance systems, and submarines.

Without computers, modern weapons could not be built, tested, deployed, or operated. All the revolutionary technologies of modern warfare, including gyros, lasers, avionics, nucleonics, and propulsion systems are dependent on computers.

Has this prevented Big Business from providing America's enemies with computers and other sophisticated equipment? Not on your life.

● During the 1970s, Control Data sold communist countries 40 systems and established a joint operation with communist Rumania. That operation is expanding to make software, integrated circuits, and peripheral equipment.

● Control Data provided the Soviet nuclear research facility in Dubna (near Moscow) with its second- and third-generation computers and pressed to permit exports to the Soviet Union of some of the world's largest and most advanced scientific computers.

● The United States continued to license sales of computer parts for the Zil truck factory long after intelligence reports indicated that the plant was turning out missile launchers.

● Among the computers IBM has sold to the Soviet Union and its satellites is the largest industrial computer in the world, at the Kama River truck plant.

● IBM computers 360 and 370 are believed to be a mainstay of the Warsaw Pact's air defense system. The complex of Western manufactured radar devices and computers in Moscow's Vnukovo Airport traffic control system can accurately project the future flight paths of airplanes and missiles, thus giving the Soviet air defense control capabilities far beyond that which the Soviets could have designed themselves.

Other firms selling computer equipment, know-how, or manufacturing capability to the Soviet block include Singer, Dataproducts, and Willi Passer.

Particularly frightening is the fact that the Soviets have apparently used our computer technology to develop laser weapons such as one used recently to blind a U.S. observation satellite. As defense expert Miles Costick wrote: "In my presence, the former chief legal counsel of the contracting division in the Soviet Ministry of Armaments gave a sworn statement that, without the use of American computers, precision instruments and digital tools in Soviet research and development laboratories, the Soviet military-industrial complex could not have made any advances in the development of high-energy lasers or nuclear devices."

The communists, whose economic system discourages innovation and invention, are totally dependent on the West for computers. Our capacity for mass production, quality control, software, memory capacity, and overall creativity far surpasses anything that can be achieved outside a free economic system.

In the typical year of fiscal 1979, computers accounted for 40 percent of all Eastern block export licenses approved by the Commerce Department and reviewed by the Defense Department. But computers aren't the only high-tech equipment Americans sell to the Soviets.

● Lockheed sold the Soviets an RB-211 turbo-fan engine suitable for bombers. The engine was developed with $300 million in grants from the U.S. government.

● Technology from Litton Industries makes it possible for Soviet planes and ships to track American submarines.

● In 1972, the Bryant Chucking Grinder Company of Springfield, Vermont, sold 164 of its unique precision grinding machines to the Soviets for $6.5 million. These Centralign-B machines are of critical importance in the grinding of ball bearings, which are used to guide intercontinental ballistic missiles (ICBMs). In order to defend the U.S. against resulting improvements in the Soviet missile guidance system, it was necessary for President Reagan to approve the MX missile program with a price tag of $15 to $20 billion—

costing the taxpayers up to 3,000 times what the Soviets paid for the machines.

A strong military needs not just high technology items, but also a whole industrial infrastructure. In 1971, the official magazine of the Soviet army, *Red Star*, reported, "In this era of complex weapons systems, all of heavy industry—from steel to electronics—and not only pure defense industries producing military end products, represents the foundation of military power."

The Soviets have long recognized the importance of automotive transportation to their military efforts. In 1927 the official Soviet newspaper *Pravda* reported, "If we do not develop our automotive industry, we are threatened with the heaviest losses, if not defeats, in a future war."

Eighty American firms helped build the Kama River Truck Plant mentioned above. With an annual production capacity of 150,000 to 200,000 ten-ton multiple axle trucks, the plant has a greater capacity than all U.S. heavy-duty truck manufacturers combined. Among the companies involved was the Swindell-Dresser Company, which provided technologies that are revolutionizing Soviet industry.

Although the Soviets promised not to use the trucks for military purposes, they were in fact used by the Soviet army in its invasion and occupation of Afghanistan, where it gassed and killed hundreds of thousands of men, women, and children.

U.S. businesses are just as helpful when it comes to naval forces. That point was unwittingly made by Richard Nixon in 1972.

To justify his blockade of Haiphong Harbor during the Vietnam War, President Nixon released photos showing the Soviet cargo vessel *Michurin* steaming toward Haiphong with rows of Soviet trucks filling it to the gunwales. What Nixon didn't mention was that the diesel engine that powered the *Michurin* was designed and built in the United States, as are the engines for countless other Soviet vessels.

Not only do we sell the Soviets equipment they used for military purposes, but also we have trained hundreds of their technicians in connection with those sales of equipment. Meanwhile, Soviet citizens have toured defense-related U.S. plants under the pretext of doing business. A member of a Soviet group that closely inspected Boeing, Lockheed, and McDonnell-Douglas factories in 1973 and 1974 confided to a Boeing official that no purchases had been contemplated, that the reason for the inspections was to learn more about the plants' operations.

The attitude of many international business people toward trade with the Soviets is summed up by Control Data president William Norris' remark that "Our biggest problem isn't the Soviets; it's the damn Defense Department."

President Reagan's appointee to chair the Export Board, Sperry-Rand chief executive J. Paul Lyet, shares this view. Asked by *U.S. News and World Report* whether the U.S. should use trade as a weapon against the Soviets, he replied, "I'm just a businessman trying to make a living—and so you may think this is self-serving—but I would think that trade builds bridges.

"I don't subscribe to the Russian system. But eventually there's going to be a coming together—peaceful coexistence, if you want to call it that. I think that the more their people see our system and how it works, the more it's going to moderate their views. . . . I would like to assume that economic growth in the Soviet Union will lead—even if slowly—toward more freedom for the people of that country as well as a more accommodating attitude toward world peace."

When President Carter cancelled the sale to the Soviet propaganda agency Tass of a computer made by Sperry-Rand, Lyet reacted far more emotionally. Scoffing at the idea that such a computer might be used to aid the Soviets in spying on dissidents, he snapped, ''I say bah humbug to that. That's like saying that if you sell trucks, the trucks can be used to haul dissidents off. If you sell rope, the rope can be used to tie up dissidents.''

At least Lyet showed some understanding about what the Soviets do with the products we sell them.

U.S. businesses have also pushed frantically for the right to help the Soviets build the Yamal pipeline, a 3,500-mile engineering marvel that will cost $10 billion. The pipeline will carry trillions of cubic feet of natural gas annually from icy Siberia to Western Russia and to Europe.

Soviet technology was not up to the task of constructing the pipeline, so Free World businesses were awarded some of the fattest construction contracts in history to help with the job.

U.S. industry alone will earn about $1 billion, with Dresser Industries, Hughes Tool, General Electric, and Caterpillar Tractor as the principal beneficiaries. Other firms that benefit from the deal include Detroit Diesel Allison Division of General Motors, Baker International of Orange County, California, and Cooper Industries of Texas.

Nice as the deal is for some businesses, it's even sweeter for the Soviets. The West finances the construction of the pipeline and gets repaid not in hard currency but in the gas the pipeline moves.

That is, *if* the Soviets decide to keep the gas flowing. The Soviets have shown no reluctance to use their energy resources as an instrument of foreign policy, as Yugoslavia discovered in 1948, Finland in 1958, Albania in 1961, Red China in 1962, and Cuba in 1968. More recently, the Soviets threatened to cut off oil to Poland unless the government cracked down on the Solidarity movement.

Once the pipeline is finished, West Germany is supposed to get 38 percent of its gas supply from the Soviets, France 35 percent, and Italy 30 percent. As Western Europe becomes dependent on the Soviet gas, it will be even more willing to accommodate the Soviet Union.

The pipeline peddlers argue that, if Western Europe's supply of gas were cut off, it would switch to Norwegian gas. That is absurd. Most of the Soviet gas will go directly to home cooking and heating, and the half-year required to bring Norwegian gas on line would be totally unacceptable politically to the threatened NATO governments.

Not only will the pipeline render Western European nations extremely vulnerable to Soviet pressure, but also it will help the Soviets solve their own energy problems.

Soviet petroleum production has leveled off. The largest operating coal mines are nearly exhausted, and 75 percent of reserves are in regions thousands of miles from the bulk of consumers in Eastern Russia. At least 100 of the country's 300 producing gas fields have passed peak production, and new areas for exploration are virtually inaccessible.

That's where U.S. big business comes in. Because there are almost no roads or railways in Siberia, the Soviets need Western-produced, high-quality, large-diameter pipe and pumps to transport their gas westward.

By providing these things, our Western industrialists will, with a single project, solve the Soviets' energy shortage and simultaneously put Western Europe under the Soviet thumb. And the West is financing this deal!

Big business' support for Marxist regimes extend beyond just the Soviet Union and Eastern Europe, of course. For example, the support of Gulf Oil has been indispensable to the communists in Angola.

Richard K. Kolb wrote in *Human Events* in May 1982 that "Gulf Oil, which accounts for 80 percent of Angola's oil output, . . . keeps the country's economy afloat. In 1980 alone, Gulf poured $325 million in taxes and royalties into [Angola] coffers. Angola's petroleum minister openly ad-

mitted that 'There is a war. Most of the profit is eaten up
by the war.'"

At that time, according to the Heritage Foundation, Gulf
Oil paid Angola $5 million a day—$3 million of which went
to the military or to repay the country's debt to Cuba and
the USSR.

Kolb wrote, "When the MPLA was fighting for power,
Gulf Oil reportedly paid the Marxists $1 million a month
to keep the war away from the oil-producing enclave of
Cabinda. Since then, the Cubans have apparently been neg-
ligent in protecting Gulf's investment.

"At one point, the Front for the Liberation of the Enclave
of Cabinda forced a reduction of oil production by 15 to 20
percent. A rebel attack recently crippled the refinery which
supplies all of Angola's domestic petroleum needs. No wonder that Gulf opposes U.S. aid to pro-Western forces."

No wonder that, in 1981, Gulf executives lobbied and
testified against efforts to repeal the Clark Amendment,
which bans U.S. aid to the pro-democratic forces attempting
to liberate Angola. As an executive of another oil company,
P.W.J. Wood of Cities Service, put it, "It's up to the
Angolans to change things in their country if they want to,
not us."

It's a shame the Soviets and Cubans don't have the same
attitude as P.W.J. Wood; the citizens of Angola might be
free now, instead of communist slaves. Unfortunately, Wood
is not the only corporate executive who thinks there is nothing wrong with doing business with the communists, thereby
providing financial assistance to communist aggression.

As Lenin is supposed to have said, "When the time comes
to hang the capitalists, they will gladly sell us the rope with
which to do it."

When big business helps communist dictatorships, ad-
vertises on immoral television programs, and lobbies for
special treatment under the law, it is taking unfair advantage

of society. If it has any responsibility to the common good, it must at least follow the old advice to physicians in the Hippocratic Oath—''Above all, . . . do no harm.''

By continuing to show disregard for the economic, social and defense concerns and interests of all Americans, big business is an important factor contributing to the growth of the populist movement.

4 / Big Banks

Imagine you are a senior loan officer at a middle size national bank in Anytown, U.S.A. One day a swarthy gentleman with a Latin accent, in a rather sly demeanor, presents himself at your desk. "Buenos dias, Señor," he says. "Allow me to introduce myself. I am Fidel Martinez Cruz, Finance Minister of the People's Revolutionary Republic of Nicaragua. I am here to become your customer. My government wishes to borrow 25 million Yankee dollars to finance our revolution."

This may not have been just what you expected on a Monday morning but, being courteous, you decide to hear this out.

"Ah yes, Nicaragua," you say. "Didn't you people overthrow that dictator Somoza in 1979, and promise free elections and human rights and the free press and that sort of thing?"

"Certainly, Señor. But right now let us discuss the 25 million dollars."

"Well, as I recall, didn't President Carter get Congress to agree to lend you fellas $75 million in 1980, as a gesture of support for your democratic revolution and all that sort of thing?"

"Actually, Señor, President Carter was very good to us. But, you see, it is very expensive to clean up after a revolution. There are a lot of arms to buy, and police to train, necessary expenses, no? And we inherited a lot of debts from the old regime. We need the money to pay some interest coming due soon, and we certainly hope your bank will cooperate with us."

"You need the money to pay just interest? What about repaying the principal?"

"Come now, amigo, we are a sovereign nation. Therefore, we are not expected to repay principal. We just borrow what we need to make the interest payment."

"Tell me, then," you continue. "Just what rate of interest do you expect to pay on this loan?"

"Well, the London Inter-Bank rate is over 12% right now, but we pay only 7%. The difference is just added on to the principal, you know."

"Hmmmmm. You know, our bank has been trying to lend to the local businesses here in Anytown. Interest rates are up around 15%, that makes it tough on them, and on our farmers and home buyers. I really don't think we could put our money out to you people for half the going rate of interest, especially when you tell me you never pay back the principal, nor even all of the interest. And I must say that I have heard some rather poor reports about you Sandinistas. Whatever became of those elections you promised? And what about your building the most powerful army in Central America? And taking your orders from Fidel Castro and the Soviets? And shutting down your only free newspaper? And confiscating private property? And sending guerillas into El Salvador? You know, I hope you won't mind my saying this, but the people here in Anytown would have a bloody fit if we took their deposits and shipped them off to Nicaragua on any terms, let alone on the ridiculous terms you propose!"

The Sandinistan visitor is unperturbed. "Very well, amigo, we gave you your chance to make some real money, but obviously this is a very reactionary thing. So you should know that we don't need your bank to make this loan. We will get the money, on just the terms we seek, from your Bank of America. So, '¡Vaya con Dios, amigo!'"

The hypothetical Sr. Martinez was, of course, quite right. The Bank of America syndicated precisely this loan for the Marxist regime of Nicaragua in December, 1982—long after it had become perfectly clear that it had become the spearhead for Soviet penetration of Central America.

Banking is a necessary part of any modern economy. Some way must be found to collect idle savings and lend them out to enterprises that create jobs, profits, and new wealth. Most banks in the United States perform just this role. They finance the small businesses and the farms and the home purchases in their towns and counties. For a fee, they accumulate and supply the loan capital to make the process of economic development go forward.

But throughout our history, there have always been those who have seized upon the legitimate functions of banking as a way of financing wild speculations, or issuing bank notes of dubious value, or, in modern times, making unsound loans on the principle of easy profit splurge, and taxpayer rescue later. All of these schemes have sought to make big profits for the insiders at the expense of everyone else.

The Jeffersonians of the early 1800s generally feared and opposed banks. They saw them as engines of fraud which would be manipulated in the service of special privilege, and against the interest of the farmer, mechanic, and artisan. In 1816, Thomas Jefferson wrote his friend, George Logan: "I hope we shall crush in its birth the aristocracy of the monied corporations"—meaning the banks—"which dare already to challenge our government and bid defiance to the laws of our country."

Twenty years later, a popular President named Andrew Jackson destroyed the Bank of the United States, which he saw as the instrument of the monied elite for robbing the common working man. Hard money was as much of an obsession for Old Hickory as it had been for Mr. Jefferson. "Check the paper mania and its corrupting consequences, and the republic is safe," wrote Jackson to Martin Van Buren, his beleagured successor amid the bank panic of 1837.

The kind of abuses perpetrated by irresponsible banks in the 19th century had largely disappeared in the 20th. Securities laws inhibit the promotion of overvalued stock by banks and other corporations. The function of issuing small denomination bank notes has been taken over by the Federal Reserve System. Today, depositers are insured to $100,000 in almost every bank in the country. Most smaller banks are not in the position to do much damage to society. Most of them do a great deal of good in collecting capital from the many and concentrating it to finance economic development and housing in their community.

The threat to the ordinary citizen from banks in the last 12 years has come increasingly from the wildly irresponsible lending policies of the big money center banks—chief among them David Rockefeller's Chase Manhattan, Citibank, The Bank of America, and the other giants. In a wild scramble for profits and market share, these big banks have made billions of dollars in initially profitable but economically unjustifiable loans. Then, when those loans have begun to go sour, the big banks expect the taxpayers to bail them out.

When a country bank lends money to a shoe store, and the store goes broke, the bank must write off that loan and swallow the loss. That is the normal risk of banking. But when a big bank makes a loan of millions, even billions, of dollars to a major corporation or governmental agency or, foreign government, it does not seriously expect to lose its money.

The shoe store in San Diego may fail, and no one but its owners and employees, their families and the store's creditors will suffer, but when a huge corporation threatens to fail, the management and its bankers are on the first plane to Washington. They want the government to inject new funds to keep their enterprise alive. Or, at worst, they want the taxpayer to be made to share as much of the grief as they can get the government to shift to his shoulders.

Over the past dozen years, the big banks have honed this technique to a real art form, and, every time, the little guy has had to pay, pay, pay. Unless a lot of little guys get mad enough to put a stop to it, a lot of such payments will yet be made.

By 1970, the Lockheed Corporation was in serious trouble with its L-1011 air bus. Despite being the nation's largest defense contractor, there was a real possibility that it would be forced into insolvency. Its bankers, who laid out $400 million to keep the company afloat, did not like the idea of losing their money.

So Lockheed, its management, stockholders, bankers, and labor union, descended upon Washington. They pointed to the dire consequences of Lockheed's failure: 31,000 jobs wiped out overnight, suppliers bankrupt, national security endangered, etc. Mindful of an approaching national election, the Nixon Administration gave Lockheed a warm welcome. Treasury Secretary John B. Connally engineered a Lockheed bailout plan whereby the federal government guaranteed $250 million in new loans to the company. That proved enough to do the job. Armed with new defense contracts, the government had a powerful incentive to make sure that Lockheed had a lot of business and Lockheed worked its way out of the hole by 1977. The bankers breathed a sigh of relief. So did the taxpayers.

The next big bailout was New York City. For years it had lavished benefits and subsidies upon its public employees, its poor, and its not so poor. Worse, it had juggled its books to hide the true extent of its fiscal irresponsibilities. Future income was listed as cash in hand. Today's liabilities were pushed into the remote future. As investigative reporter Ken Auletta described it, New York City's "rollover, false revenue estimates and plain lies had robbed taxpayers of literally billions through excessive borrowing to cover up excessive fraud."

New York City subsidy levels were astonishing. The city hired 49 employees per 1,000 residents, compared to 30 to 32 in virtually all other major cities. The salaries of these New York City employees far outstripped those of their counterparts elsewhere. For example, a porter employed by the city earned $203 a week, while a private sector x-ray technician earned $187. Subway change makers earned $212 a week and never changed anything larger than a ten dollar bill. Bank tellers, whose duties are much more varied than those of the municipal employees, averaged $154 a week, and municipal fringe benefits packages were twice as big as those of other public and private employees in New York state.

Even today, the city continues to offer free college education to any city high school graduate at the City University of New York (CUNY). At the time of the crunch, CUNY cost the city $500 million a year. The city ran a large number of public hospitals, most of them significantly underutilized and overstaffed. It also operated 130 middle income housing projects at a large loss. Each apartment was subsidized at a rate of $150 a month. Keeping the subway fare well below the actual cost was an article of faith for any aspiring New York City politician. In actively and creatively featherbedding public projects and institutions to provide permanent and high paid jobs for an ever growing number of middle class service providers, New York City was almost unique.

Where did New York get the money to pay for this runaway wasteful spending and misdirected subsidies? From taxes, of course—and from the usual begging of transfer payments from Albany and Washington. But, increasingly, as its finances worsened, New York City sold its debts to banks and bond markets.

By the end of 1974, New York City was trying to sell $600 million worth of bonds a month to stay afloat. In that year, the city went to the bond market eight times. The bond market began to get suspicious. When the city tried to pressure its employee retirement trust into buying the cities debts, investors started to head for the hills. In February, 1975, practically no one wanted anything to do with New York City's debts. The City was on the brink of bankruptcy.

Naturally, what passed as the city's political leadership was in a state of hysteria; so were public employee unions. And so were New York's big banks.

At that point, the banks held some $2 billion of the City's debts. With $400 million, David Rockefeller's Chase Manhattan led the way; City Corp followed with $340 million.

So one might ask, how did these great banking houses end up with $2 billion worth of the debt of a city rushing head-long into financial oblivion? Where were the shrewd bankers? The auditors? The accountants? The endless checks imposed on the lowliest shopkeeper seeking to borrow $10,000 to remodel his store? None was to be found. Even as the City squandered billions right under their noses, the big banks simply shoveled out more and more money. They apparently asked no hard questions, demanded no references, sought no cosigners, required no business plans. They just handed out the money and had their pictures taken with the Mayor—until the dark day the roof caved in.

When the day of reckoning arrived, did the big banks

denounce in shocked tones the carelessness of the city? Did
they point to suddenly discovered waste and extravagance
all around them and demand a new era of fiscal responsibility? Not at all.

Instead, the big banks simply joined the chorus of politicians and other malfactors demanding a federal rescue. It
wasn't even the total amount of money that drove the banks
to do so. Their total exposure was less than 1% of their
assets. The Federal Reserve Board estimated that only six
of the nation's 4,700 banks would be in any danger if the
city formally defaulted.

In a devastating chapter in his book, *A Time for Truth,*
Treasury Secretary William E. Simon recounted how New
York City's bankers told him time and again that the only
responsible remedy for the city was bankruptcy, followed
by a supervised workout and radical change in its spending,
subsidizing, and accounting methods.

When it came to saying it publicly, however, the bankers
turned chicken. They joined in demanding a federal bailout.
David Rockefeller even enlisted West German Chancellor
Helmut Schmidt to urge the Congress of the United States
to rescue New York City. Herr Schmidt did so dutifully at
a planeside news conference, predicting an international
financial calamity if the City's pleas went unheeded. (Later,
when it no longer mattered, Herr Schmidt apologized in
person for what he had done.)

So, once again, Washington hastened to bail out the big
banks that had made the bad loans. In December, 1975,
Congress passed a bill authorizing Treasury loans to New
York City of up to $2.3 billion, with city and state revenues
earmarked to assure repayment. The strict terms were due
largely to the presence of Secretary Simon. The ink was
hardly dry for the big bailout when the banks were back for
yet another one: this time, for the Chrysler Corporation. In
a nutshell, Chrysler had continued to build cars as if there

had been no OPEC oil embargo. It had assumed that soaring gas prices would have little to do with customer demands for fuel-efficient vehicles. By 1978, Chrysler was on the rocks. Its management was worried. Its unions were worried. And, of course, its bankers were worried.

They all got together and came up with the usual remedy: a taxpayer bailout.

By this time, however, Congress was getting a little tougher about bailing out dying corporations. It did pass a bill allowing the Treasury to guarantee up to $1.5 billion in new bank loans to Chrysler. But the Carter Administration wanted to minimize its exposure. So Treasury Secretary G. William Miller put the screws on Chrysler creditors to accept 30 cents on the dollar in order to retire over $600 million in debts and to accept preferred stock in return for $700 million.

Despite this substantial write down, Chrysler's banks avoided the even more serious problem of outright default and, needless to say, the bankers were enthusiastic advocates of the federal bailout.

Thanks to the federal loan guarantee, Chrysler, by 1980, was able to float loans at 10.35%. At the same time, Ford, its competitor, had to pay 13.50% for loans. It stands to reason that Chrysler should have paid at least 4 percentage points as a guarantee to the federal government. But it didn't. It paid only 1%. Taxpayers are absorbing the wide difference—and Ford is suffering from the subsidized competition from the firm which, two years earlier, should have been auctioned off to its more farsighted competitors and to new, more dynamic, job-creating companies.

All three of the bailouts I've mentioned—Lockheed, New York City, and Chrysler—worked to the advantage of the big banks who lend hundreds of millions to big cities and big corporations. In each case the banks, although strong advocates of the bailout, were not the prime movers.

In their domestic lending, the banks have been far less

irresponsible than in their foreign lending of the late 1970s. It is here that the full enormity of the big bank ripoff really begins to go out into the open.

The beginnings of the foreign binge of the 1970s came with the OPEC oil embargo of 1973, and the skyrocketing increase of oil prices thereafter. The effect of these phenomena was the transfer of hundreds of billions of dollars from American consumers to OPEC treasuries.

Some OPEC countries such as Nigeria and Venezuela had plenty of things upon which to spend their new found wealth. Others, like the thinly populated Arab states, didn't know what to do with it all. For various political and cultural reasons, they were reluctant to purchase real assets in Western countries. Instead, they invested their surplus in Western banks. Almost overnight, Western banks found themselves sitting on billions of deposits bearing interest.

To a bank, the deposit is not an asset but a liability. It is the business of banks to lend out deposits at a higher rate of interest than they pay depositors. So the major banks scrambled to find borrowers for all these new deposits. A Chase Manhattan could, of course, set its loan officers scouring the countryside to offer loans to worthy borrowers, businesses, and homebuyers. But that is costly and difficult. The prohibition against interstate branch banking also limited opportunity. So Chase continued to service prime customers such as Lockheed, New York City, and Chrysler; but, clearly, some major new outlet was needed to absorb all the petrodollar influx.

The big international banks found that outlet in huge new loans to foreign governments. Despite scores of examples of defaults to private banks by foreign governments dating back to 1927, the big bankers widely assumed that loans to governments could not go bad. Someone would always pay. If not the government, surely some international lending institution would step in to make them whole—or a foreign country would extend its financial umbrella to a troubled borrower, as the U.S.S.R. did for the Poland government. Or, as a last resort, the U.S. government would come to the rescue with public credits or taxpayers' dollars.

Furthermore, it was easy to lend to foreign governments. Since it was assumed that the borrowers could always pay ("governments don't go out of business"), it wasn't necessary for the banks to ask too many questions. As Zbigniew Brzezinski was later to put it: "These credits were given on a helter skelter basis without sufficient information, without a data base, which even a small personal loan is subject to in Western society."

Bank agents swarmed over foreign capital, trying to unload their quota of bank loans. They were very successful: by 1982 the non-OPEC developing countries owed $520 billion. Of that, at least $182 billion was owed to banks—and $108 billion of it to U.S. banks. The nine largest U.S. banks had lent $60.3 billion—over 220% of their capital—to the 40 major non-OPEC developing countries. Over half of that amount had gone to the three largest: Mexico, Brazil, and Argentina.

As the 70s came to a close, it began to look, increasingly, as if a lot of borrowers would not even be able to pay the interest; so the bailout began.

The first was to Panama. In 1970, the Panamanian government decided to make Panama a banking haven. It practically abolished foreign bank regulations and instituted a Swiss-like secrecy about banking transactions (much appreciated by those engaged in the Colombian drug traffic). In return for throwing open Panama City to foreign banks, the Panamanian government expected loans. It got them.

After a while, banks began to wonder how Panama would repay the loans. Panama had one great money-making asset: our Canal. If the Canal were turned over to Panama, Panama could raise the toll to pay off the banks. Thus began the pressure for transferring control of the American Canal to Panama.

One of the diplomats, Ellsworth Bunker, was a former director of Bankers Trust Company of New York. The other was Sol Linowitz, a major stockholder and board member of Gray Midland Bank, to which Panama owed at least $8 million. Interestingly, President Carter gave Linowitz only a six month temporary appointment in order to avoid Senate confirmation hearings which might have produced a lot of embarrassing information about Linowitz's bank connections. It was not until Congressman George Hansen (R-Idaho) and Senator James McClure (R-Idaho) filed suit for a temporary restraining order that Linowitz resigned his bank position.

The progress of the Canal giveaway negotiations and the all-out Senate battle for ratification of the Carter treaty has been told elsewhere. With the notable exception of Senator Orrin Hatch (R-Utah), Senator Jesse Helms (R-North Carolina), and the late Jim Allen (D-Alabama), opponents were not supposed to understand why the big American banks were so eager to see our great asset transferred to a corrupt, left-wing Latin American dictatorship.

But a popular radio commentator and once-and-future presidential candidate named Ronald Reagan would question whether the big banks might have put prepayment ahead of any concern for national security. On November 1, 1977, his concern was answered definitively. In *The New York Times* that day appeared a full page advertisement paid for by the "Committee of Americans for the Canal Treaty." Among the signers: David Rockefeller, John J. McCloy of Chase Manhattan, Ben Heineman of First National of Chicago, Board Member Irving Shapiro of Citibank, and other representatives of the international banking community. Also among the signers, incidentally, was George P. Shultz of the Bechtel Corporation. Four years later, Ronald Reagan, who had led the national fight against the Canal Treaty, named Shultz his Secretary of State.

The treaty was narrowly ratified by the Senate, the Canal tolls were raised, and the die was cast. Other Latin American countries denounced the United States for the higher toll. So much for the theory of "winning friends in Latin America by giving away our Canal."

A year after the Panama Canal Treaty rescued the banks in Central America, the Iranian hostage crisis burst upon the world. Although the fact was overshadowed by public concern for the hostages in Tehran, that, too, contained a strong ingredient of bank bailout. Thanks to the diligent work of Congressman George Hansen and Financial Journalist Mark Hulbert, we know a lot about Chase Manhattan's central role in the Iranian crisis. It is a long, tangled story, but the outlines can be simply related.

David Rockefeller's Chase was the personal bank of the Shah of Iran. As such, it is much reviled by the revolutionary regime which, in 1979, overthrew the Shah.

In the mid-70's, Chase had syndicated a $300 million loan to the Shah. The Iranian constitution required that such loan be approved by the Majlis (parliament). But the Shah had so little use, even for his own hand picked-parliament that he neglected to secure its rubber stamp.

The loan was completed anyway, although the Chase's Iranian counsel warned that it probably was not legal. When the Ayatollah Khomeini gained power, the Chase began to suspect that the new government might use illegality as an excuse to repudiate the loan from the Shah's favorite banker.

It seemed that the Chase could get its money back only if discord between the United States and Iran grew more serious. If the U.S. government were to freeze the Iranian accounts in this country so that they could not be withdrawn by Iran, and if Iran repudiated the loan, the Chase could seize the Iranian deposits and begin the long process of litigation to obtain as much repayment of its loan as it could.

Then came a lucky break for Iran's creditors. David Rockefeller and his diplomatic counselor, Henry Kissinger, arranged to have the Shah admitted to the United States. He came in for medical treatment, but the sole physician who insisted that the treatment be given in the United States was David Rockefeller's personal physician, sent to the Shah's villa in Mexico for that purpose.

When the Shah arrived in the United States, reaction was swift in Tehran. The students seized the Embassy and took 52 hostages. Ten days later, Iranian Finance Minister Bani Sadr announced the withdrawal of Iranian deposits, primarily from the Chase. Early the next morning, Jimmy Carter signed the order freezing Iranian deposits.

Meanwhile, on November 5, the Iranian Central Bank routinely cabled the Chase to transfer funds for oil sales accounts to make payment on the $300 million loan due November 15. By the 15th, however, Jimmy Carter had frozen the assets, and the Chase claimed it could not take Iran's funds out of one account and apply it to the debt in another. Thus, Iran was in default on its loan. The Chase and everyone else then entered into a massive scramble to attach all available Iranian assets.

In due course, after the hostages had spent a visible year in captivity, a settlement was reached. Significantly, releasing the hostages was only a minor part of the settlement. The main part was to settle accounts with Iran to the benefit of American banks.

The resolution of the Iranian hostage incident was not to be the end of the bank rescue operations. There came, in 1982, still another—to Poland, which, a year earlier, had been the scene of terrific political ferment. The independent trade union, Solidarity, which, in the Western sense, was more a political movement than a union, showed signs of seriously undermining the Marxist-Leninist dictatorship. At the same time, Poland's economy slipped over the brink toward complete bankruptcy.

By January, 1982, the Polish regime was committed to making a $71 million payment to American banks which had financed the sale of feed grains to Poland. The banks made use of a Commodity Credit Corporation guarantee program through which the Department of Agriculture promised to make good in case of foreign government default.

The procedure was straightforward: banks documented the default, and the CCC wrote them a check. The declaration of default, however, would have caused a major problem for the same big banks. Poland was $26 billion in debt to the West. Although U.S. banks held less than $2 billion of that debt, their European counterparts, particularly in West Germany, were much more exposed. A declaration of default on one transaction would trigger cross default clauses, in effect throwing all of Poland's foreign debt into default.

Since Poland, unlike Iran, had few assets within reach of a Western court attachment, a full scale default would require prompt writedown of billions of dollars in loans which the banks were carrying at face value, even though everyone on Wall Street knew they were virtually worthless.

Of course, as *Time* magazine would say later, the banks showed Poland "far more lenience than that given to a laid-off Detroit auto worker if he missed a few payments on his wife's washing machine."

So the banks again asked for rescue operations. Through the Treasury Department, they persuaded the Agriculture Department to make good on the guarantee without requiring the declaration of default.

This outrageous case of rule twisting caused a rebellion in the Senate. Thanks to Senator Robert Kasten (R-Wisconsin), Congress eventually prohibited any further fulfillment of CCC guarantee unless the banks involved formally declared a default. In the meantime, however, while the

Reagan Administration worked to stall Senate action, over $400 million was paid out to banks without any requirement of the dreaded declaration of default. Once again the banks got their cash without embarrassment.

Finally, we come to the granddaddy bank bailout of them all: its outlines are not fully clear, at least to the public, but its key intermediate step is an increase in the lending capacity of the International Monetary Fund.

The IMF was created in 1946 as a result of the Bretton Woods conference. That was an era when the dollar was tied to gold, and the major currencies of war-torn Europe were linked to the dollar through a fixed exchange rate.

Under such assistance, there is a need for the temporary financing of balance of payments deficits, while the country involved takes steps to remedy economic problems. Otherwise, the trading countries would be forced into repeated currency devaluations, with a serious adverse effect on world trade. This temporary financing to maintain exchange rates was the purpose of the IMF.

In 1971, however, after a decade of economic mismanagement, the United States closed the gold window and refused to swap one ounce of gold for every $35 turned in by foreign central banks. From that point on, the dollar has had no tangible backing whatsoever. With no financial anchor, the world's various currencies began to float against each other, depending upon market forces.

At this point, all rationale for IMF loans evaporated. But the IMF bureaucracy, and the big banks which were their constituents, had no intention of going out of business. They decided to become, in so far as possible, a world central bank. The IMF would go on making loans and giving economic advice to countries in trouble, just like the U.S. Federal Reserve Board would do for a distressed domestic bank.

The existence of the IMF relieved some of the anxiety of

the international banks which had made irresponsible loans to countries sinking ever deeper into trouble, such as Mexico, Brazil, Argentina, the Philippines, Sudan, Zaire, Tanzania, Hungary, Yugoslavia, and Romania. (The U.S.S.R. and Poland do not belong to the IMF.) IMF loans open the possibility of debtor countries using the funds to pay off the loans to the banks. That, however, was not what usually happened; the main purpose of IMF lending has been to keep borrowers afloat until the final bailout could be effected.

The IMF gets its funds from 146 member countries in the form of national currency subscriptions in exchange for the IMF's Special Drawing Rights (SDRs). Most of the national currencies are virtually worthless outside the issuing country (and sometimes within it). Only the yen, the dollar, the pound, the Deutsche mark, and a few other Western currencies are in demand by IMF borrowers.

From time to time—usually every five years—member nations are asked to increase their contributions. By 1978, however, it had become apparent that 1980 was too long to wait. So the IMF invented a $10 billion supplementary financing facility. The Carter Administration obligingly drove a subscription bill for this through Congress and Carter then got Congress to approve yet another quota increase.

Today, however, the funds are running out faster and faster. So, completely contrary to President Reagan's longstanding convictions about free enterprise, his Administration caved in: it asked Congress to approve another $8.4 billion for the IMF. The bill passed the Senate easily, but, running into strong opposition from both liberals and conservatives in the House, it squeaked through on a narrow 217 to 211 vote in August, 1983, after a strenuous battle, as a majority of the President's own Republicans voted against him.

The next time you go to the polls, try to remember whether

your Congressman and Senators supported the IMF bailout. Before you vote, consider the fact that, of the IMF's 1,525 employees, 20 percent make more than $100,000 a year.

The greatest danger in the big banks' influence on our nation's politics lies in the fact that they have no concept of patriotism nor national security; nor do they have any compunction about making loans wherever they think they can find a profit.

Thomas Theobald, Vice President of Citicorp, was questioned in 1981 about his bank's loans to Poland: Did he feel nervous about making a loan to an oppressive communist regime which, a week earlier, had imposed martial law to suppress its free trade unions? Not at all.

"Who knows which political system works?" he responded. "The only test we care about is, can they pay their bills?"

Equally candid, at least on one occasion, was David Rockefeller himself, freshly returned from Marxist Angola. Was he bashful about lending to Angola? Not at all.

"I don't think an international bank such as ours ought to try to set itself as a judge about what kind of government a country wishes to have. We have found that we can deal with just about any kind of government, provided that they are orderly and responsible."

The government he was dealing with in Marxist Angola was using David Rockefeller's loans, Gulf Oil's $5 million a day, and 20,000 Cubans to wage a war against the pro-American forces of Jonas Savimbi. Presumably they were doing so in an "orderly and responsible way." At the United Nations, that same government distinguished itself by being one of the handful of states to oppose the resolution condemning the Soviet invasion of Afghanistan. The same attitude shows in the remark of an unnamed executive of a major New York bank, as reported in the *Wall Street Journal* of December 21, 1981: "Most bankers think authoritarian governments are good because they impose discipline. Every time there is a coup d'etat in Latin America, there is much rejoicing and knocking at the door offering credit.''

Paul McCarthy of Chemical Bank reinforced that view on the McNeil-Lehrer Report during the Polish Solidarity struggle in 1981. ''Worker self-management,'' he said, ''would be counterproductive. In my opinion what is needed for the immediate term is greater centralization.'' Presumably Mr. McCarthy was relieved when General Wojciech Jaruzelski imposed martial law a few weeks later.

The role of these same banks in financing communism is notorious. Rockefeller's Chase Manhattan financed 45 percent of the Kama River Truck Plant in the Soviet Union. Most recently Kama trucks have become common in Afghanistan, as they were earlier in the streets of Hanoi. The Bank of America headed the syndicate that channeled another $25 million to Marxist Nicaragua in December, 1982, even as the Reagan Administration was spending many times that to defeat Nicaragua's efforts to further Soviet penetration of all of Central America.

What should be done about all this? The details may prove complex, but the principles are simple.

No more bailouts; no more shifting of burdens from the big banks to the innocent worker and taxpayer.

No more government guarantees of loans to foreign borrowers, particularly foreign governments and their entities.

No more U.S. contributions to the IMF.

No more government fulfillment of existing loan guarantees in the absence of declaration of default.

No more loopholes to allow the Federal Reserve to rescue careless bankers by monetizing foreign debt.

It is tragic that this is not the policy of the Reagan Administration. But an aroused America can make it a policy in future administrations.

5 / Big Unions

Who speaks for the working person? *Unions,* the establishment would answer. But the fact is that unions often operate in the interest of their leaders, rather than their members.

One reason for this is the undemocratic way in which many unions are organized. In some ways, union "democracy" has more in common with one-party rule in totalitarian countries than with the multi-party systems common to the Free World.

When was the last time you heard that an entrenched union leadership was defeated in an election? In most unions, the leadership continues from year to year, monopolizing communication within the union and choosing its own successors.

By keeping their members under strict control, the unions are able to maximize their ability to fix prices, to increase their own wages at the expense of other workers.

Thirty years ago economist Milton Friedman estimated that, by enforcing a monopoly on certain types of labor, 10 to 15 percent of the work force is able to increase its wages by 10 to 15 percent, at the expense of the remaining 85 to 90 percent of workers (whose wages are about four percent below what they would have been). More recent studies have indicated the relationship remains about the same.

Price fixing does not work in a truly free economy. But U.S. law makes it possible for unions to fix prices by several methods.

For example, the law gives a union the right to represent workers who are not members, especially in states that do not have Right to Work laws. A plant unionized by a majority vote many years ago may remain unionized simply because no one has the courage to stand up to the union. And federal rules make it difficult to decertify a union, although decertification is, in fact, happening more and more often.

Another way the law enables unions to fix prices is the "prevailing wage" law. In federally funded construction projects, the Davis Bacon Act usually requires that union rates be paid, enabling the unions to fix the price of labor for those projects. When a contractor is given a choice between hiring union workers, who are usually the best trained (because the unions monopolize training programs), and hiring non-union workers, he will usually hire the union worker—if the non-union worker is prohibited from selling his labor at a lower price. Another consideration that may influence the decision is the fact that contractors who hire non-union labor sometimes find their tires slashed.

Violence, and intimidation by the threat of violence, is another way unions can benefit financially at the expense of society. Of course, unions deny that violence and threats play a significant role in their relationship with management. But if that is true, why have they worked overtime to defeat anti-extortion laws?

The Hobbs Anti-Extortion Act of 1951 made any extortion or robbery that interfered with interstate commerce a federal crime. But in 1973, the Supreme Court ruled 5 to 4 that union violence in pursuit of "legitimate union goals" was exempt from that law. Efforts by Republicans in the Senate to reverse that decision have been stymied by the unions.

Why? Because many unions depend on violence to maintain their monopoly over labor in a particular industry or region. The National Right to Work Legal Defense Foundation uncovered 2,500 reports of union violence between 1975 and 1982.

At a Senate Judiciary Committee hearing in October, 1983, a dozen witnesses testified about the need to apply the Hobbs Act to unions. Cher Mungovan of Hawaii testified that her husband was forced to establish a new identity, under the federal government's witness protection program, after he testified against Carpenters Union officials charged with perjury. She said she had no idea where her husband was; she did not join him "underground" in order to defend suits against them by the union.

Because of union violence, Mrs.Mungovan said, their business had been destroyed, their creditors were foreclosing on their home, and their 12-year-old son was undergoing psychiatric counseling.

Is violence really necessary to achieve so-called "legitimate union goals"? William Winpisinger, President of the International Association of Machinists and Aerospace Workers, was quoted in *Time* magazine in 1978: "In my lifetime, no group has ever gotten justice in this country without lawlessness. So if we want to see change, then we may have to stop having such a high regard for law and order."

Unions also become undemocratic in order to present a united front on political issues. Dissent from the official "party line" on important issues would weaken the union's ability to elect its friends and intimidate its enemies.

Today, we have come to associate unions with left-wing politics, with socialism, with support for centralized planning of the economy. But for many years union leaders were less interested in rubbing elbows with the rich and powerful and more concerned about the economic interests of their members. They favored a system which allowed workers to join together to offer their services to employers through the free marketplace, because they knew such a system would benefit the politically powerless.

The principal weapons used by management to suppress unions were injunctions issued by anti-labor courts. Unions knew that, in a free economy, they would be allowed to organize, bargain collectively, and strike when they could not reach agreement with management. In a free economy, no one is required to work for a wage he does not freely accept.

Political scientist V.O. Key wrote in *Parties, Politics, and Pressure Groups,* that "Over a long period the AFL insisted . . . that its true doctrine was *laissez faire*: let the state leave labor alone; it would care for itself through organization, collective bargaining, and the strike. Government intervention was frowned upon, since it might deprive labor of its freedom to employ the economic weapons at its command."

Few groups are entirely consistent in their views, and labor was no exception. Unions loudly proclaimed their support for economic freedom at the same time they sought restrictions on immigration and discriminatory laws against women. But for the most part they only asked government to get out of the way—to stop using convict labor to drive down wages, to stop issuing injunctions against strikes, and so forth.

According to Key, the first marked change in the philosophy occurred in the railroad unions. It is somehow fitting that the industry most responsible for the partnership of big business and big government also moved unions in the same direction. (See the chapter on "Big Business.")

It is notable that the railroad unions sought government intervention only *after* the government began to regulate the industry. Once rates were regulated, it was only a matter of time before the railroads' costs—including labor costs—would be regulated as well.

It took many years for the libertarian economics of the labor movement to shift toward the left. It was not until 1932 that the AFL reversed its position against compulsory unemployment insurance. It was not until 1939 that the federation's president, William Green, declared that "We now seek benefit for the workers and all our fellow men by the use of either direct economic strength or legislation as the situation demands. Neither alone can suffice."

Gradually, unions became involved in issues far beyond wages and working hours. The AFL's principal competition, the Congress of Industrial Organizations, became especially political, taking positions in almost every area of government policy. After the merger of the AFL and the CIO in 1955, the trend sharply increased.

The *AFL-CIO News* annual report on Congress described the voting record of each member in terms of his support for the union. Among the proposals supported by the union in the 1981 report were the Tennessee-Tombigbee Waterway, a synthetic fuels plant boondoggle in Kentucky, the portions of the Voting Rights Act that discriminated against Southerners, the Davis-Bacon "prevailing wage" law, and a massive subsidy for the merchant marine. At the same time, the union opposed the modified Kemp-Roth tax cut passed by Congress and an anti-busing measure proposed by Senator Jesse Helms (R-N.C.).

All of the positions listed as union-approved are contrary to the interests of the American taxpayer. Most are contrary to the interests of even the most dedicated unionist. Yet the AFL-CIO persists in promoting its view as the opinion of the working man and woman.

A Pittsburgh steelworker pays his union dues so he can get a fair wage and fair benefits, not so some union leader can play politics. But tens of millions of dollars in union dues are spent every year on political causes, whether the rank and file agree with those causes or not.

Most people oppose using compulsory union dues for political activities. A 1977 Roper poll showed that 67 percent of union members and 72 percent of the general public thought the practice should be prohibited.

But in the last few years union officials have grown increasingly political (and increasingly partisan) in their use of dues money.

During the 1976 Carter-Mondale campaign, the Communication Workers of America used its members' dues for financing a direct mail program to distribute pro-Carter brochures to 307,000 CWA members; paying lost wages to rank and file CWA members who left work to campaign for Carter; and paying 113 local workers who assisted CWA's get-out-the-vote drive for Carter.

Labor columnist Victor Reisel estimates that American labor leaders spent more than $100 million to back up their endorsement of Jimmy Carter and other candidates in 1976, a hefty expenditure even out of an estimated $3.5 billion taken from compulsory dues.

The significance of that $100 million is that the entire general election campaign of the official Carter-Mondale reelection committee cost only about $40 million. Most of the union support was in the form of "in-kind" services, such as communications between unions and their members. Thus, it was not even officially counted as a "contribution."

According to Riesel, unions paid for "tens of thousands of precinct workers; for around-the-clock computer printouts of statistics on millions of members; for the 'walking around' doorbell ringers; for the phone banks, the carpools, the babysitters, the buddy-system reaching for the aged, the infirm and all who can physically make it to the polls. . . ."

In 1980, the AFL-CIO alone had 140,000 activists working for the Carter-Mondale ticket, with the union's effectiveness heightened by salaried "volunteers" and tens of millions of dollars provided by union officials from around the country.

The vast majority of union political funding comes from compulsory dues, not from voluntary contributions. There are supposed to be restrictions on the use of dues for political purposes, but union officials know how to get around the rules.

Steelabor, the publication of the United Steelworkers of America, reported in 1979 that compulsory dues "can't go for direct political contributions but . . . can do a lot: mailings supporting or opposing candidates, phone banks, precinct visits, voter registration and get-out-the-vote drives . . . and [dues] can be used to raise voluntary funds for the [steelworkers union] political action committee."

Such spending limits the unions' legitimate efforts in collective bargaining to ensure a fair wage for union members. Consider the Communications Workers of America, one of the most left-wing unions in the country.

In August, 1980, a federal court found that the CWA had used only 19 percent of its 1979 income for legitimate collective bargaining purposes. The other 81 percent—more than $24 million in 1979 alone—was used primarily on politics and internal union activities such as union leaders' travel expenses and publicity.

A court appointed official ordered CWA officials to refund the 81 percent not spent on collective bargaining to employees who challenged the union. He prohibited the CWA from collecting monthly payments in excess of the amount necessary for the expenses of collective bargaining.

But despite such court intervention and increasing dissatisfaction among the rank and file, unions are demanding more amounts from their members for political purposes. On November 12, 1981, the AFL-CIO's executive council ordered its local affiliates to increase their political contributions 42 percent by 1983.

As the government's share of the nation's wealth increases each year, the stakes grow higher. Although two out of three union members think it is wrong to use dues for politics, the union establishment thinks otherwise. In 1984 it will break all records for union participation in politics.

The link between union leaders and the left wing of the Democratic Party seems to grow stronger every day. Throughout the history of the union movement, until approximately the time of the Goldwater candidacy for president, unions regularly supported candidates of both political parties. And the candidates who received the highest ratings from union PACs were liberal on economic issues but conservative on defense. The head of political "education" for the AFL stated his union's policy very clearly in 1949: "We must ever be vigilant to keep our local leagues completely independent and nonpartisan. We must not become the tail to any political party. . . ."

However, by 1980, 93 percent of financial campaign contributions and almost all "in-kind" contributions were going to Democrats. The Senators rated highest by the unions were McGovern, Kennedy, Bayh, and others on the extreme left of the nation's political spectrum.

In October, 1983, the AFL-CIO abandoned its one-time pretense of nonpartisanship and endorsed Walter Mondale for the Democratic presidential nomination in 1984—its first pre-primary presidential endorsement. Regardless of how many members of union households voted for Ronald Reagan in 1980 (44 percent, compared to 47 percent for Carter, according to a *New York Times* survey), and regardless of how many union members may vote for a Republican, an independent, or a Democrat other than Mondale in 1984, the nation's federation of unions endorsed for president one of the most liberal figures in American politics.

The endorsement guarantees vast sums of money as well as a political machine that extends from the national level to every community in America. Most political analysts have valued the AFL-CIO pre-primary endorsement at $20 million, or half the total amount major party candidates who accept public funds can spend in the general election campaign.

Union support has a value far beyond anything that can be measured in dollars. The AFL-CIO endorsement gives the former Vice President a network of supporters in every state in the nation, in every Congressional district, and in almost every precinct.

This network helps convince union members that, if they do not support the AFL-CIO's candidate, something is wrong with them. Peer pressure is used to prevent members from acting independently. It is typical of the establishment, which sets certain opinions as reasonable and declares contrary opinions unreasonable. Thus, a large percentage of union members who indicate they will vote for a non-endorsed candidate end up following the union line on Election Day.

Besides creating a bandwagon effect for its own candidates ("Everybody *else* is for Mondale; what's wrong with you?"), the union's network prevents any other candidate from gaining momentum. Union members who are potential supporters of other candidates are intimidated into silence. And often a good potential candidate will decide not to run for office when he realizes that his union-backed opponent will have professional telephone banks and trained door-to-door campaigners working for him across the nation, state, or district.

I am not suggesting there is anything basically wrong in unions endorsing or providing support for candidates. But unions can do so legitimately only so long as they represent the views of their members; otherwise, it is just another case of the establishment taking advantage of the people.

Most union members are conservative in their politics, proudly middle class in the way they live, and increasingly fed up with union leaders who take positions they do not agree with. The ever-widening gap between union officials and union members is creating a genuine crisis in organized labor in America. If AFL-CIO President Lane Kirkland and other union officials do not make major adjustments in the way they lead, they will soon have very little to lead.

In the last few years, national union leaders supported the Panama Canal treaties, ERA, gun control, tax increases, the big bank bail out, and "affirmative action" quotas, while they opposed a constitutional amendment to balance the budget.

When 3,000 people marched on Washington in 1975 to protest court ordered busing, in a rally organized by some 60 union locals in Kentucky, the AFL-CIO repudiated the protest as a violation of union policy. When the Massachusetts AFL-CIO approved an anti-busing resolution, the national union threatened to revoke its charter.

More recently, unions have thrown their support behind "gay rights." Homosexual activists have long contended that "gays" are entitled to government protection of their life style. Not content with being left alone by government, they want to use the power of government to prohibit anyone from treating them differently because of their sexual orientation.

They want passage of a "gay rights" bill that would require the government to take action against persons who discriminate against homosexuals in employment and housing. A "gay rights" law would legalize homosexual marriage and adoption and would probably lead to quotas for the hiring of homosexuals.

If the assembly line at a plant in Saginaw voted on "gay rights," it would be doomed to failure. Many people, even those who believe the government should leave "gays" alone and let them answer only to God, are repelled by the proposal that the government require people to associate with homosexuals.

What does this have to do with unions? Simple: In their never ending quest for political power, unions have formed an alliance with homosexual activists.

In June, 1982, labor reporters wrote that "AFSCME [the American Federation of State, County, and Municipal Employees], the largest union of public employees, went on record endorsing gay civil rights, and later this year, it is expected that the full AFL-CIO will take a supportive position at Lane Kirkland's suggestion."

The month after that item appeared, AFL-CIO President Kirkland joined the rest of the Leadership Conference on Civil Rights in an unanimous vote admitting the National Gay Task Force and the Gay Rights National Lobby as participating organizations. Later in 1982, John Perkins, the AFL-CIO's Political Director, was the guest of honor at a Washington dinner sponsored by a "gay rights" political action group.

In virtually every area of public debate, the official union position is different from that held by workers. According to union analyst Dr. Dan Heldman, a plurality of union workers oppose the AFL-CIO liberal position on:

- Federal responsibility for housing.

- Welfare spending.

- Teacher strikes.

- Political contributions by unions.

- A guaranteed annual minimum income.

- Foreign aid.

- Aid to parochial schools.

Union members no longer even support their leaders on so fundamental an issue as the laws against requiring workers to join unions in order to get a job. A Roper poll in 1977 found 58 percent of workers supporting Right to Work laws and 63 percent endoring retention of Section 14(b) of the Taft-Hartley Act that allows states to adopt such laws.

In addition, 64 percent favored the limiting of picketing to a specific contractor, although the legalization of so-called "common situs" picketing has been a goal of unions for years. Such a law actually passed Congress once, only to be vetoed by President Ford, who had previously supported it.

A 1978 poll by the Opinion Research Corporation found that only 33 percent of union members supported a union-backed bill to make it easier for unions to organize, while 51 percent said they believed union leaders already had too much power. A 1981 poll by the same organization found 64 percent of the general public and 61 percent of skilled blue collar workers favored an end to unions' exemption from anti-trust laws.

An Associated Press-NBC News poll in 1981 found that 73 percent of the American people agreed with the statement, "American labor leaders are out of touch with the needs and desires of the workers they represent," while 18 percent disagreed. Among people who said that either they or some other members of their household were union members, 67 percent agreed with the statement.

Lane Kirkland has been a leading critic of attempts to trim federal spending and taxes. He has referred to the call for a balanced budget and reduced taxes as "hysteria." He has stridently opposed across the board tax cuts that are the same for everyone, preferring instead an "industrial policy" in which tax breaks would go to companies that politicians want to help. He has likened President Reagan's support for a balanced budget amendment to a "sermon on sin while molesting the choir girls."

Yet 57 percent of union members have said they favor further spending cuts, and two out of three favor tax cuts beyond the limited relief passed in 1981. In 1981, 65 percent of workers polled by the Opinion Research Corporation supported a constitutional amendment to balance the budget.

That same poll, conducted for the AFL-CIO Committee on Political Education (COPE), indicated that 72 percent of workers supported a stronger national defense. Yet throughout the Reagan administration, the AFL-CIO has united with far-left and admittedly communist organizations in protests against President Reagan's attempt to restore America's security.

In September, 1983, the AFL-CIO joined numerous anti-U.S. organizations in support of the "Jobs, Peace, and Freedom" march in Washington, D.C, which supposedly commemorated the 20th anniversary of the 1963 civil rights march. In fact, it was an attack on Reagan administration policies that supported free enterprise, an adequate national defense, and political liberty.

Among the groups participating in the demonstration were the U.S. Peace Council (the American arm of the Soviet-front World Peace Council), the Mobilization for Survival (which lists the Communist Party, USA on its masthead as an affiliate), and the Committee in Solidarity with the People of El Salvador ("People" meaning the communist rebels).

As columnist M. Stanton Evans wrote, "How did the good folks from the AFL-CIO and other respectable organizations let themselves get hooked up with such people, in such a disreputable cause?"

If George Meany were alive, I don't believe his union would have participated in such an event. Meany, an up-through-the-ranks plumber and Irish Catholic traditionalist, strongly opposed communism. He worked constantly to steer organized labor away from any connections with communists or with persons blind to the enormous evil of communism (the so-called "fellow-travelers"). Meany even steered the AFL-CIO away from the 1963 civil rights march, when his knowledge of the background of some persons involved in the demonstration outweighed his support for an end to the evil of segregation. When the Democratic Party nominated George McGovern, Meany likewise steered his union away from the McGovern campaign.

Unfortunately, as union support for the so-called "Jobs, Peace, and Freedom" march of 1983 demonstrates, union leaders have adopted a radical agenda. With increasing frequency in the last few years, they have ignored the economic interests of workers to pursue political causes opposed by their own members. I believe that is one of the major reasons for the unions' decline in recent years.

The AFL-CIO's membership has been steadily eroding. In 1955, the year of the AFL-CIO merger, the federation had 12,622,000 members, almost 8 percent of the U.S. population of 165 million. Today, it has almost the same number of members, or 5 percent of a population of some 230 million.

Employees have been rejecting union representation at an increasing rate. Over the last several years, unions have consistently failed to win representation in more than 50 percent of the elections certified by the National Labor Relations Board. Unions have not won a majority of representational elections in any year since 1973.

Recently there has been an unprecedented number of decertification elections, that is, attempts to kick the unions out. In 1981, unions lost three out of four campaigns, costing them a record 27,510 members.

A 1979 Gallup poll showed public approval of unions at its lowest point in 43 years with only 55 percent expressing approval. This compared with a high mark of 76 percent approval in 1957. In a 1981 Roper survey, only 50 percent of Americans had a great or fair amount of confidence in the ability of union leaders to make real contributions to our society.

A typically disaffected and disgusted union member is Gale Cronk of Flint, Michigan. Cronk spend almost 30 years as a United Auto Worker, serving Local 659 in various capacities. In 1978 he ran as the Republican Congressional candidate in an overwhelmingly Democratic district. His union endorsed his opponent.

What does Gale Cronk think? "If labor doesn't reappraise its position, it's going to blow the whole ball game. The union leaders and union members aren't even playing on the same team anymore. . . . If our leaders aren't representing the workers, who are they representing?"

Big union leaders ignore union members like Gale Cronk at their peril.

One final note: If there was ever a case that showed the heartlessness of the union establishment, it is the "homeworkers" case in Wisconsin.

As reported by columnist Donald Lambro, a group of women in Ripon, Wisconsin, who work to support their families by embroidering skirts and blouses in their homes, has been the victim of union collaboration with Labor Department bureaucrats.

A 1943 Labor Department regulation forbids Americans from producing six crafts in their homes for profit: embroidery, women's apparel, gloves and mittens, buttons and buckles, jewelry and handkerchiefs. President Reagan's Secretary of Labor, Raymond Donovan, eliminated a ban on knitted outerwear. But when he tried to repeal all the regulations, the International Ladies Garment Workers Union forced him to back down. Now the homeworkers face the prospect of losing their livelihood, and being forced to get on the welfare rolls because of this ridiculous regulation.

ILGWU President Sol Chaikin explained his union's position during a debate with a homeworker: "You want every worker to be free to work at home at whatever they desire to do, under whatever conditions they want to work. That's anti-social. It's wrong."

No, Mr. Chaikin, the word for it is "American."

6 / Big Education

There is a bitterness deep down in our nation today because the ordinary American, the little guy, is beginning to understand the many ways that the rich and powerful reserve for themselves and their children access to the most basic means of achieving and maintaining a good life.

A good education is one of the best roads to the good life. But, in its current state of collapse, the public school system is a raw deal for the men and women who must depend on it to educate their children. The current system, dominated by the education establishment, victimizes the children who depend on public schools for their start in life. By ensuring ignorance, it undermines democracy itself.

In 1983, a steady stream of commissions and panels made the case that public education had suffered a dangerous decline. The hue and cry began with the report of the National Commission on Excellence in Education. The theme was echoed by the Twentieth Century Fund, the Education Commission of the States, and the Carnegie Foundation for the Advancement of Teaching, among others—none of them "conservative".

The conclusions of all were basically the same, though the National Commission had the best rhetoric for it: "If an unfriendly foreign power had attempted to impose on America the mediocre educational performance that exists today, we might well have viewed it as an act of war.

"As it stands, we have allowed this to happen to ourselves. . . . We have, in effect, been committing an act of unthinking, unilateral educational disarmament. . . . While we can take justifiable pride in what our schools and colleges have historically accomplished and contributed to the United States and the well-being of its people, the educational foundations of our society are presently being eroded by a rising tide of mediocrity that threatens our very future as a Nation and a people."

The surprising thing about this and the other reports was that the public did not question their findings. For once, the media agreed with the description of the problem. The only group in America that tried to pretend that the public schools were in great shape was (guess who?) the public school establishment.

At first, it denied there was a problem. When confronted with clear evidence, the education establishment retreated to its usual theme: Give us more, more, more money. Democratic presidential candidates, keenly sensitive to the political clout of the National Education Association union, began to outbid each other in their pursuit of the endorsement of the teachers' union.

All their proposals came at a time when education was already big business. There were 2,464,688 classroom teachers in elementary and secondary schools in 1980, up from the 2,394,000 of 1975. Total national expenditures for education—including elementary, secondary, and higher education—were $199,800,000,000 in 1981, up from only $89 billion in 1972.

In recent years, education expenditures have been nearly 8 percent of the Gross National Product; back in 1929, when everyone agreed American education was doing its job, its costs were only 3.1 percent of GNP. In 1962, education took 37 cents of every dollar spent by state and local governments; in 1971, it was 39 cents.

What does this huge amount of money actually buy? It has not been paying high teacher salaries. In that, the teachers' union is at least partly correct in its complaints. Teacher salaries have declined steadily since 1959 as a proportion of the national per pupil expenditure. In that year, they accounted for 53 percent of education expenditures, but by 1979, they were less than 40 percent. When adjusted for inflation, teacher salaries have fallen since 1970, and now just about match the national average for all occupations (about $18,000 per year).

During the 1970s, something interesting happened to student teacher ratios. The number of students enrolled in public schools K-12 in 1970 was 44,983,062. These students had 2,387,000 teachers. By 1980, the enrollment had dropped to 40,984,093, with 2,553,694 teachers. In other words, four million fewer students had 166,000 more teachers. Put in economic terms, the productivity of the teachers had fallen noticeably. When anyone else's productivity falls, they do not expect to get raises. Considering that teachers teach less than 200 days a year, their salaries are not so low as might be thought from a quick look at the numbers.

Nevertheless, it is evident that many bright, competent, dedicated people are not attracted to teaching. Teaching is viewed as a bottom-of-the-heap job. The 1982 Scholastic Aptitude Test scores of students desiring to be teachers were 80 points below the national average.

Not even literacy can be assumed: California recently put into place a minimum competency test to ensure basic skills in new teachers, and one-third of the first 7,000 to take the test failed it. In previous years, those people would have been teaching, whether they had the basic skills competency or not.

But there is more to being a good teacher than being able to read and write English. Mastery of the subject is high on the list of important qualities. A sense of self-respect, which will translate into calm control over the classroom, is essential, since today's teacher will encounter every stage of rebelliousness, hostility, and emotional disorder, thanks to the ongoing breakdown of the family.

A good teacher is willing, even eager, to involve parents. A 1983 survey funded by the National Institute of Education found that parents, teachers, principals, and educators all had a favorable attitude toward parental involvement—up to a point: When queried about their attitudes toward parental involvement in areas such as text books, curricula, and evaluation of pupils, the teachers became more negative regarding parental involvement.

The selection of curricula is particularly loaded with controversy, since many of the conflicts in the schools rage over curriculum content. When parents get "too" effective, they are branded as book burners by the education establishment. When Mel and Norma Gabler of Texas became effective in influencing the school textbook selection process in their state, they were made the object of a national hate campaign by People for the American Way.

You didn't hear much about teachers until recent times. A few years ago, the image of teachers was of stern, no-nonsense men and women who instilled discipline and knowledge with a firm hand, and won the everlasting gratitude of their students. Today, the complaining, despairing, unsuccessful teacher is the unfortunate, mostly false stereotype.

It so happens that the steady decline in student performance has taken place since federal funds become available in large amounts for the supposed improvement of education.

The real infusion of federal money came with the enactment of the Elementary and Secondary Education Act (ESEA) in 1964. Prior to ESEA, the financing of education was a local concern, and local bond issues had to be defendable and practical, because they were locally accountable. State money was subject to essentially the same conditions.

Then federal money became easily available. ESEA encouraged the education establishment to expand and experiment to its heart's content. Federal grants for education rarely, if ever, required evidence of progress or improved student learning. It made no difference whether a project was a success or failure—the money would be given, and given again, just for meeting the right criteria.

Not all teachers were eligible for federal bounty. Only those with proper club memberships, the "professionals in good standing", would be considered for the programs available. Under the claim of protecting the public from quackery, the "professional" dominance of federally sponsored programs was ensured.

Thus, ESEA gave the professional education establishment an important boost. "Professional" theorists and strategists created their own little laboratories for educational experiments. The changes they brought about have been primarily responsible for the decline in the quality of American education, for the disintegration of the system of local control, and for the gradual decline of support for public schools.

In Washington, D.C., as in state capitals, Big Education is a bureaucracy, a lobby, and a pressure group. In local districts, it is the administrators whose advice school boards generally seek and follow. In teachers' colleges, the local establishment designs the courses and directs the placement office.

The education establishment has labored long and hard to create the illusion that there are great mysteries to teaching, that only persons who have been trained as "professional educators" can teach. It claims that "teaching is a highly complex endeavor involving ever greater techniques and never ending knowledge of the highest order. . . . Teaching requires continuous education to be relevant to the needs of the practitioner. . . . Teaching assumes the need to have a supportive staff of specialists for the teacher to draw upon at all times for assistance.''

The result of this attitude has been rapid growth in the number of teaching degrees awarded each year. In 1950, 61,000 bachelor's degrees and less than 21,000 master's degrees were awarded in the field of education. In 1980, colleges handed out 118,000 bachelor's degrees in education and 103,000 master's degrees.

The education establishment makes every effort to exclude from teaching anyone with expertise in a different discipline—anyone who might challenge the ideology of groups like the NEA. That's why requirements for certification include a large number of ''method'' courses rather than content courses—it's easier to indoctrinate students in the nebulous ''method'' courses. No one can attain certification without passing through that indoctrination.

The establishment's stated goal is ''professional self- governance'': ''It is pure myth that classroom teachers can ever be held accountable, with justice, under existing conditions,'' argued former NEA President Helen Bain.

''The classroom teacher has either too little control or no control over the factors which might render accountability either feasible or fair,'' she said.

What are the demands of the education establishment?

1) Authority over issues, suspending, revoking, and reinstating the legal licenses of educational personnel. That is, the teachers' unions want total control over who is allowed to teach. State laws to require minimum competency exams for aspiring teachers would be impossible if the education profession had this measure of self-governance.

2) Authority to establish and administer standards of

professional practice and ethics for all educational personnel, independent of the concerns of parents.

3) Authority to accredit teacher training institutions. Already, state laws governing accreditation are generally written on the recommendation of the state bureaucrats. The regional and national accreditation bodies are also manned by members of the establishment.

4) Authority to govern in-service and continuing education for teachers. Although access to, and preparation for, the profession may be controlled, once teachers are on their own in a classroom, they may find themselves thinking independently, or succumbing to conservative influences. To combat this danger, in-service education and the network of teacher centers will help keep them in the fold.

It is significant that the kind of courses which qualify for in-service training are not the content-oriented courses. Few content courses are available, but there are many "method" courses. In other words, to advance as a teacher, don't learn how to speak French, take the course in "How to *Teach* French."

All the militancy of this self-styled "profession" would not be terribly important for the nation, were it not for the degree to which the education establishment can control the direction of the country by influencing our children.

The National Education Association concerns itself mainly with its own selfish interests and with influencing national politics. State legislators who are otherwise staunch conservatives quake in their boots at the prospect of antagonizing the NEA.

At its annual meetings, the NEA adopts resolutions urging all teachers to "devote at least 10 hours" to campaigning for NEA-backed candidates. That kind of volunteer power pays dividends for an organization that claims 1.7 million members, 600 employees at its national headquarters, and a budget of $250 million. In 1980, 464 delegates to the

Democratic National Convention were NEA members; it was the largest single bloc of votes.

But despite its heavy political involvement, NEA claims to promote impartiality and fairness in the classroom. The amazing thing is that the public has only recently begun to question NEA's sincerity.

In 1982, the NEA published a curriculum which viciously attacked the conservative movement. Shortly thereafter, it published *Choices: A Unit on Conflict and Nuclear War*, which vigorously advocated a nuclear freeze. No less a liberal organ than *The Washington Post* editorialized against *Choices*. And the liberal *New Republic* said that NEA, "rather than campaigning for better education, has spent its time and money campaigning for political candidates in hopes of accumulating power. The movement," said the magazine, is running the "Department of Education, a bureaucratic honeypot for education special interest."

NEA does more for the nuclear freeze movement than just publishing study units on it. Former NEA Executive Director Terry Herndon was a leader in forming a 33-group coalition called Citizens Against Nuclear War. Under his leadership, NEA endorsed STOP, the Student Teacher Organization to Prevent Nuclear War, a front group for anti-nuclear organizing. At the 1982 NEA Convention, members and affiliates were urged to create local units of STOP. An NEA staffer was assigned to work exclusively on so-called "peace" projects, with 53 NEA affiliates and "peace" organizations abroad.

A cynic might ask whether it is more important for the NEA to promote unilateral disarmament than to spend its time giving reading skills to inner city youths, in order to free them from a future dependence on welfare and crime.

Reviewing the NEA Legislative Program for the 98th Congress, a cynic might wonder whether the NEA is very interested in education at all. Some Program samples:

- ''NEA opposes the misnamed 'Family Protection Act.' '

- ''Draft registration should be based on equal responsibility for men and women.

- ''Legislation should be enacted to prohibit smoking in public places.

- ''No U.S. military or economic assistance shall be given to any foreign government which violates or permits the violation of the basic rights of its citizens. For example, NEA shall work for cessation of aid to the current administrations of Guatemala and El Salvador. [They, of course, do not refer to communist countries in which citizens have absolutely no rights.]

- ''Legislation should be enacted proclaiming an annual National Women's History Week.

- ''Mandatory national health insurance should be enacted and should be provided by public and private agencies to assure health services.

- ''The federal government should assist state and local communities in improving and expanding child care services
. . .

- ''Right to work laws must be opposed and section 14(b) of the Taft-Hartley Act should be repealed. Any weakening of the minimum wage will be opposed.

- ''Restrictive provisions of the Hatch Act should be removed.

- ''The Communications Act should be revised to reflect a stronger emphasis on the public interest, fairness doctrine, equal-time requirements . . . Financial support must be provided for public broadcasting . . .

- ''Antitrust laws should be enacted and enforced to prevent oil companies from expanding into alternate forms of energy.

● ''NEA supports the concept of the Kennedy-Hatfield nuclear arms freeze resolution as introduced in the 97th Congress.''

Of course, NEA is not totally oblivious to its supposedly primary function of education. Some of its agenda reflects a concern for teaching and learning, but on its terms:

● ''Standardized tests should not be used to deny students full access to equal opportunity or to evaluate teachers . . .

● ''Bilingual and English-as-a-second-language (ESL) programs are unique and necessary to achieve . . . and so should be funded sufficiently to be available to all students not proficient in English.

● ''Legislation should be enacted to provide comprehensive guidance and counseling programs for elementary students . . .

● ''NEA will be vigilant in striving to secure re-authorizations of all federal educational legislation and other legislation of concern to the organization.

● ''The goal of national security through peace can be achieved only by the education of the citizenry to compete and succeed in a complex and interdependent world. Therefore the proposed disproportionate allocation of funds increasing the national defense budget and decreasing federal funding for education must be reversed.''

Reviewing the space devoted by the National Education Association to the issues it considers important, it is clear the bulletin sent to teachers from a local chapter of the Oregon Education Association was right on target when it stated: ''The major purpose of our association is not the education of children, rather it is, or ought to be, the extension and/or preservation of our members' rights. We earnestly care about the kids and learning, but it is secondary to the other goals.''

When the failure of the education establishment is loudly proclaimed by liberal and conservative alike, you wonder why the arguments and demands of a self-centered teachers' union should be given such weight in the making of public policy.

The first step toward ending establishment control of the educational system is an end to NEA's privileged position as the organization that determines the priorities of our schools.

NEA's most important asset is its captive audience of tens of millions of students each day. Because average daily attendance figures (''a.d.a.'') are used to determine federal and state aid, the whole education establishment is geared up to maximizing the ''a.d.a.'' There are constant campaigns for lowering the age of mandatory school attendance—even in the face of clear evidence of the actual harm that academic training can do to children, especially boys, at ages below six or seven. There are demands for lower pupil-teacher ratios, although studies have indicated little relationship between class size and academic performance.

After liberating children from the control of the education establishment, we should open teaching to people whose principal field of study has been biology, or trigonometry, or English literature, and we should deemphasize degrees in education.

We should change the requirements for teacher certification to encourage more content study. Promotion, pay raise, and hiring policies should be altered to reflect teacher ability, not just seniority, and we must establish merit pay systems. In addition, we should establish tougher literacy standards for teachers.

It may be that we will have to increase teachers' salaries in order to attract good people—but the costs can be made up elsewhere from some of the frills that will disappear when good teaching returns. To attract good teachers, there is another factor at least as important as money: administrators, parents, and the courts must support discipline and the authority of the classroom teacher.

At the federal level, several measures would help. First, we must stop the flow of money to "innovative" education schemes, teacher centers and other vehicles of indoctrination. Abolishing the federal Department of Education would diminish the power of the establishment, but most of the necessary steps can be taken at the state level, through such actions as returning authority to the local districts. Otherwise, local control of public education will soon be nothing more than a fast-fading memory.

It should be made clear that our educational problems stem from the control of an establishment elite led by the National Education Association and the U.S. Department of Education. The average schoolteacher, as an individual, is generally not a part of this conglomerate, but only its tool.

Most classroom teachers are only vaguely aware of the left-wing positions their union takes. Those who join it do so in some cases because they have no choice—they don't live in a Right to Work state—or because of the necessary benefits NEA membership offers. With 1.7 million members, the organization can provide discounts on subscriptions, vacations, and liability insurance. In many public schools, teachers need special insurance, but school boards generally cannot or will not pay for it.

Even with a large membership virtually assured, NEA fears competition for itself or for the schools it dominates. Otherwise, why would it pass resolutions demanding that closed public schools not be sold or rented to other institutions of education?

There have always been non-public schools, of course—

in fact, government-funded schools were mostly unknown in the United States until the 19th century. Until recent times, private schools fell into two categories: Elite prep or finishing schools, where the wealthy sent their children to acquire social graces, make the right friends, and prepare to excel at Ivy League colleges—or Catholic parochial schools—low-budget, community-centered operations which perpetuated the Catholic faith. While other religious denominations had their own parochial schools, non-Catholic religious schools were comparatively rare.

In 1980, there were five million students in private elementary and secondary schools. Only 800,000 of them were in non-religious schools, and only three million of them were in Catholic schools. Most of the rest were in non-Catholic Christian schools.

The education establishment senses in the Christian schools its most serious competition. NEA vehemently opposes any form of aid or relief, such as tuition tax credits or vouchers, to help private school parents bear their burden of double taxation. NEA predicts that, if parents of private school students received aid, the result would be the destruction of public education. NEA perpetuates the stereotype of Christian schools as the last refuge of bigots and racists, and demands that government regulate and control all private schools, regardless of whether they in fact practice racism.

In 1983, the freedom of religious schools was seriously compromised by the U.S. Supreme Court's decision in the Bob Jones case. The Court ruled that it is unconstitutional for a school (in this case, a college) to receive a tax exemption if that school's religious policy conflicts with government policy. Bob Jones University forbade interracial dating, but did not discriminate in admissions.

Later in the same year, a district court ruled that Georgetown University, a Catholic institution, could refuse to grant official status to a campus homosexual club—on the very slim grounds that no federal policy of non-discrimination against homosexuals had *yet* been defined. The implication was clear, that when a federal policy is defined, the right of a religious school to practice its beliefs will cease to exist if those beliefs are inconsistent with government policy.

The precedent of the Bob Jones and Georgetown cases—that a religious school wanting tax-exempt status cannot practice a doctrine contrary to government policy—is alarming to anyone who wishes to see our First Amendment freedoms preserved. But it is a logical outgrowth of government efforts to eliminate dissent in the area of education.

Most Christian schools are small and financed on a shoestring. Typically, one is organized by born-again evangelical or fundamentalist parents and churches. It may be organized by one church or by several churches.

Nobody really knows how many such schools there are, nor how many students they enroll. Federal statistics are not completely reliable, because many fundamentalist schools refuse to fill out any forms for federal agencies, and have never been adequately surveyed. But based on government figures, Dr. Ron Godwin, director of the Moral Majority, estimates there are about 19,000-20,000 private Protestant schools with some two million students. Various experts estimate that new Christian schools are being founded at the rate of three a day.

Part of the reason for the growth of Christian schools is a loss of confidence in the public schools. Each year the annual Gallup Poll on attitudes toward education finds a greater percentage of public school parents willing to shift their children to private schools if they can afford it. The figure is above fifty percent.

With teachers more concerned about teaching than politics, with discipline and higher academic standards, Christian schools are very attractive to many concerned parents. Of course, the existence of these schools is a slap in the face of the education establishment, which claims that education cannot achieve quality without vast amounts of government money.

But even if the public schools returned to the basics, it is likely that Christian schools would continue to grow. The ethics of Christian schools, on which everything from student conduct rules to teacher selection to textbook choices is based, are different from the ethics of the secular public schools.

Parents are rediscovering traditional values. They are finding out that Christian schools are the only place children can get a curriculum that admits the existence of God and seeks to fulfill His expectations for us. As long as the NEA propaganda puts Christian fundamentalists in the same category as the Ku Klux Klan, as long as the principles of secular humanism dominate teaching in the public schools, many parents are going to seek alternatives to educate their children, regardless of cost.

Colleges face many of the same problems as high schools, including grade inflation. The enormous attendance at college (nearly 42 percent of all Americans between 18 and 24 attend college, up from 26 percent in 1963) is itself both the cause and the result of grade inflation. A high school diploma does not equip one to achieve much, so more people are entering college. In response, colleges are becoming more oriented to teaching vocational skills, and academic standards are declining.

Even the cream-of-the-crop Ivy League institutions have remedial reading and writing courses. Because high schools are not doing their jobs, more people every year are forced to go to college to acquire an adequate education, and the demand for space at college has escalated.

Over the last two decades states created more public colleges in response to demand, but the action stimulated the demand for more. Twenty years ago, there were 1,409 private colleges and 821 public colleges in the United States. Now there are 1,241 public and 1,585 private colleges. Of those that closed between 1960 and 1980, 204 were private and only 36 were public.

Whether a college is public or private, its faculty may be dominated by the radical left. For example, the chairman of the economics department at the American University is a Marxist, as is half the economics faculty at the University of Massachusetts at Amherst. The explosion of "women's studies" courses would be laughable but for the use of such classes to promote radical politics.

It is interesting that the radicalization of the faculty is occurring at a time when students are becoming more career-oriented and far less ideological than the preceding generation. The campus radicals of the 60's are still the campus radicals, except that now they're on the other side of the desk.

With the cost of a year at a public college $3000 per year, and nearly $5000 at a private college, few parents are thrilled at the thought of their children being indoctrinated in Marxism and other "alternative" value systems. At some colleges, the standards of morality are such that a student requesting housing in an all-girls dorm is assumed to be a lesbian.

Thankfully, there is more freedom of choice in the selection of a college than there is at the high school level. There is a greater variety of colleges available: Christian, traditional, technical, large or small, rural or urban, innovative, liberal arts, or Great Books. The largest growing segment of the college student population, by the way, is aged 30 and older, so it is not just parents of teenagers who choose colleges these days.

Not since Sputnik has the nation been engaged in such a debate over the quality of education as it is today. Parents are demanding a return to basics, more discipline, and more serious courses, and virtually everyone outside the education establishment agrees with these goals.

Confronted with statistics showing declining achievement, the establishment responds by crying for money. But, reform first, money later, should be the taxpayer's response.

The schools should not be laboratories for social experimentation. Their purpose is to educate our children in the traditions, language, history, values, and accomplishments of our civilization and our nation.

Beyond the simple task of providing a good education, schools are not supposed to remedy the social and economic ills of society. They are not delivery systems for welfare programs. It is true that people have come to rely on the schools to perform these functions, but that must change.

After all, parents know and want what is best for their children. Reforming education in this country means breaking the monopoly control of the establishment and replacing it with parent power in every school district in the land.

The NEA distributes a bumper sticker that proclaims: "If you can read this, thank a teacher."

I would add: "If you can't, blame the education establishment."

7 / Big Law

The modern legal establishment is an alliance of judges, lawyers, and Big Government. Its power grew from the increasing feeling of Americans that every desirable end ought to be converted into a *right*. And it grew because of those in the courts who litigate increasingly to extend every judicial precedent to its "logical" end.

Our society has become what several legal scholars have called a "litigious society."

Marshall Breger, a visiting fellow at the Heritage Foundation, said that today "If one is injured one assumes that one must automatically receive redress or compensation. The welfare state mentality can only reinforce this attitude."

Breger added: "Lawsuits against a minister for giving bad spiritual advice, against a teacher for failing to teach you to read, against a parent because you turn out to be a juvenile delinquent, really are expressions of resentment against the fact that one has failed to find happiness and satisfaction in the modern world."

One of our wisest political leaders understood the terrible social costs that could arise in a society which turned to the courts to solve every conceivable problem. Abraham Lincoln once said, "Discourage litigation. Persuade your neighbors to compromise when you can. Point out to them how the nominal winner is often the real loser in fees, expenses, and waste of time.''

There is no doubt *who* benefits from the litigious society. The power of lawyers and unelected, unaccountable, judges increases every time our legislators quietly submit to yet another surrender of the people's power to them.

The sustained growth in litigation, and in the total number of lawyers, has no precedent in our history. In 1960 there was one lawyer for every 632 Americans. By 1970, there was one for every 572 persons. Today, there is one lawyer for every 375 persons in the country. In the United States, there are some 610,000 lawyers, two-thirds of the world's total.

No one is certain what this staggering number of attorneys costs the country in lost productivity and misallocation of resources. As William K. Coblentz, a San Francisco lawyer, put it, ''For every hundred lawyers who hang out their shingles or rewrite advertsing copy at the Federal Trade Commission or join big firms and go on 'document searches' or invent new theories by which to prosecute people for acts that weren't criminal before, we lost a number of biologists and doctors and engineers and presidents of efficient automobile companies.'' He concluded: ''When more of our best young brains begin to prefer producing to litigating, we will all be better off.''

Derek C. Bok of Harvard University recently noted, ''In Japan, a country only half our size, 30 percent more engineers graduate each year than in all of the United States. But Japan boasts a total of less than 15,000 lawyers, while American universities graduate 35,000 *every year*. . . . As the Japanese put it, 'Engineers make the pie grow larger; lawyers only decide how to carve it up.' ''

The benefits of the litigious society flow to attorneys not only in increased power but also in measurable dollars and cents. One of the outrageous "Catch 22" rackets perpetrated upon the average American by the legal elite is the system of awarding attorneys' fees completely out of line with the actual time and expense involved.

Through judicial awards of attorneys' fees to left-wing litigators, the federal government and medium-to-large corporations have become important sources of leftist political funding. The usual mechanism for funding liberal organizations has been a class action suit, followed by an attorney's fee request submitted to a sympathetic judge.

How does this work? *The Wall Street Journal* has noted: "The Sierra Club last February [1982] lost a lawsuit it brought against the Environmental Protection Agency to tighten pollution controls on coal-fired power plants. Nonetheless, the court ordered the government to pay the club about $90,000 in attorneys' fees because it had 'substantially contributed to the goals of the Clean Air Act.' The case is only one of dozens every year in which the government pays for legal costs even when the plaintiffs lose."

Indeed, the Office of Management and Budget estimated that in FY 1982 alone, the federal government would be forced to pay $400 *million* in attorneys' fees.

Imagine the impact the awards of such attorneys' fees have on smaller government jurisdictions. In October of 1983, U.S. District Judge Jackson Kiser, who had earlier ruled that Bible classes held in Bristol, Virginia, were unconstitutional because they were financed and operated by a private religious group, added insult to injury by awarding a stunning $25,300 in lawyers' fees and costs to the American Civil Liberties Union. Who will pay these costs? You guessed it—the people of Bristol, Virginia.

We can all sympathize with litigants who seek redress for some genuine wrong or serious health hazard created by negligence of a business. But a Rand Corporation study of 24,000 lawsuits filed by victims of asbestos contamination found that "63 cents of every dollar paid by manufacturers and insurers to settle the claims went to lawyers' fees and court costs."

No less than 120 federal statutes authorize the payment of attorneys' fees to successful litigants, and the courts have been steadily expanding the awards to unsuccessful litigants.

It is the liberal "public interest" attorneys who bring class action suits and qualify for court-awarded attorneys' fees who reap the windfall of the modern legal structure.

Another primary beneficiary in the legal establishment is the organized bar. The American Bar Association (ABA) has, in recent years, taken the lead on a variety of hard-left activist causes, losing much of its right to call itself a non-partisan, professional organization. (I recognize that, in the state bars and in some of the committees of the ABA House of Delegates, there remain pockets of populist strength.)

The ABA has opposed all efforts by populists and conservatives in the Congress to curb the excesses, abuses and outright illegalities of the Legal Services Corporation. The ABA's increasingly liberal standards assisted Jimmy Carter in elevating scores of underqualified liberals to the federal bench.

In recent years, the ABA has urged decriminalization of marijuana, advocated pro-homosexual legislation, and supported taxpayer funding of abortion on demand. In cases before the Supreme Court, the ABA regularly intervenes on the side of increased court involvement in everyday life and on the side of criminals.

The most disheartening recent activity of the ABA was the decision of its House of Delegates to squelch a much needed set of reforms designed to protect the rights of the innocent and of society as a whole. In February, 1983, ABA reformers proposed that lawyers be required to "blow the whistle" on clients they *knew* to be engaged in fraud, or on other crimes, when it came to the attention of the attorney that he or she had unwittingly been used to assist in criminal activity.

Not only did the ABA reject the reform by a 207-129 vote, the organization went on to "strengthen" the existing code to *require*, not just permit, lawyers to "keep secret all criminal activities their clients tell them about, short of a plan to commit murder or cause serious bodily injury."

Is it any wonder that popular attitudes toward the legal profession have deteriorated so dramatically in recent years? A 1983 Gallup Poll found that only 24 percent of those surveyed rated lawyers high or very high for honesty and ethics. Another 43 percent rated them average, while 27 percent rated them low or very low.

Frivolous lawsuits filed for purposes of intimidation or extortion (a code of "ethics" used as a license to protect the guilty), shady, amoral or immoral tactics designed to benefit only the guilty. These, and much more, are the legacy of the steady turn of American law away from its origins in the Judeo-Christian ethic.

The *Wall Street Journal's* Stephen Wermiel noted the shady tactics employed by criminal defense lawyers. Alan Dershowitz, a Harvard Law School professor and well-known criminal attorney, described how he deliberately asked misleading questions and tricked a detective during cross-examination. Dershowitz bluntly asserts, "I do not apologize for (or feel guilty about) helping to let a murderer go free— even though I realize that someday one of my clients may go out to kill again."

Such contempt for right and wrong has a devastating effect on how the law is applied. It leads too many lawyers to engage in money grabbing and unscrupulous activities designed solely for profit and fame. But an even greater problem in our legal system today is the incredible power of federal judges.

Protected by life tenure, federal judges have handed down

rulings which have overturned laws enacted by the Congress of the United States.

Consider these examples of what has happened to our nation and its moral and social fabric as a result of such judicial law making:

● Federal District Court Judge George L. Hart decided in 1983 to require all private schools in Mississippi to conduct affirmative action programs. He ruled that the school operated by Clarksdale Baptist Church, which does not practice racial discrimination and which teaches that racism is forbidden by Biblical precepts, must engage in an affirmative action program or lose its tax exempt status and right to receive tax deductible contributions.

What was his reason? There was "an inference of present discrimination against blacks" by "all Mississippi private schools established at or about the time public schools were desegrated in the 1960s." To refute this inference, all private schools in Mississippi must expend funds on affirmative action programs *to prove they do not discriminate*.

In other words, the court will hold private schools guilty until they can prove otherwise—the reverse of the historic American concept of presumed innocence until proven guilty.

● The New Mexico legislature passed a statute allowing a minute of silence in public schools "for contemplation, meditation or prayer," but it was declared unconstitutional by a U.S. District Court. Reasoned the court: "The ill lies in the public perception of the moment of silence as a devotional exercise. If the public perceives the state to have approved a daily devotional exercise in public school classrooms, the effect of the state's action is the advancement of religion."

● The Students for voluntary School Prayer club at Guilderland High School in Albany, New York, wanted to use an empty classroom to hold a meeting where members could pray before school. They sought recognition on the same basis as other student clubs. The principal refused their simple request. When the students sued the school, the federal court ruled in favor of the principal, reasoning that the meeting would have violated the First Amendment's establishment clause which "requires" the separation of church and state. In other words, fair treatment and equal access for students who believe in God violates the Constitution.

● At Cumberland High School in Rhode Island, Aaron Fricke, a self-professed homosexual, wanted to take his male lover to the high school prom. When the principal refused to sell Fricke tickets, Fricke sued the school, claiming he was being denied his right of freedom of speech. Holding that Fricke should be permitted to take his homosexual lover to the prom, the court said: "Even a legitimate interest in school discipline does not outweigh a student's right to peacefully express his views in an appropriate time, place and manner."

● In Washington, D.C. another Federal District judge decided that it was wrong to permit the use of paraquat to destroy marijuana plants. When the Drug Enforcement Administration (DEA) began spraying the herbicide paraquat to destroy illegal marijuana plants, Judge June Green ordered DEA to stop the spraying immediately. Agreeing with the arguments of pro-marijuana groups and some environmentalits, the judge deprived the Government of the United States of an effective weapon against the production of illegal marijuana by ruling the weapon illegal.

The Supreme Court has played the leading role in undermining the traditions of our law.

The classic case of Supreme Court legislation rather than interpretation is *Roe v. Wade*. The *Roe* case swept away nearly two centuries of constitutional interpretation and common law tradition affording substantial protection to unborn children.

It established a national pro-abortion policy. As a result, 1.5 million unborn children are destroyed every year. This single case, more than any other, exposes the myth that the Supreme Court is the great protector of minority rights. What minority is more helpless, innocent and vulnerable than unborn children?

But *Roe* is not the only outrageous Supreme Court decision. The Court took God out of American public school classrooms in *Engel vs. Vitale*, which outlawed the saying of traditional prayers in public schools, and in *Abington v. Schempp*, which forbade even Bible readings and the saying of the Lord's Prayer.

Despite the precedent of *Brown v. Board of Education of Topeka*, which outlawed the consideration of race in public policy, the Supreme Court moved to impose forced busing in *Green v. County School Board* and *Swann v. Charlotte-Mecklenberg*. These cases allowed public officials to consider race in assigning school children for forced busing.

The Supreme Court approved affirmative action quotas in college admissions, reversing its stand in *Bakke v. the Board of Regents of the University of California at Davis*. In the *Weber* case, the Court gave consent to quotas in private business hiring and job training programs.

The Supreme Court created the most notorious new criminal justice policies which have undermined effective law enforcement. In *Mapp v. Ohio*, the High Court outlawed the use of any evidence ''improperly obtained,'' even when a defendant was clearly guilty.

In *Miranda v. Arizona*, the Court ordered law enforcement officials to advise accused criminals of all their rights and threw out all confessions by defendants who did not specifically waive the right to have an attorney present during questioning.

In short, the Supreme Court has created radical new "constitutional" rights while undermining or overturning traditional rights. More than any other institution in our society, the Supreme Court has created a legal climate in which God is not allowed in our public schools and the rights of criminals outweigh the rights of victims and the rights of society.

The harsh reality of the application of the *Mapp* "exclusionary rule" is seen in the case of *Coolidge v. New Hampshire*.

On January 13, 1964, 14-year-old Pamela Mason left her house to go baby-sitting and disappeared. Eight days later she was found in a snowdrift. She had been shot in the head. Edward Coolidge's car matched the description of a car seen near the time and area where Pamela was last seen. Later, particles were found in the car which matched Pamela's clothing. Coolidge owned several guns, one of which was proved the murder weapon.

The State Attorney General issued a warrant to arrest Coolidge and a warrant to search his car. In 1971, the U.S. Supreme Court held that the search of the car was unreasonable because the Attorney General was not a neutral and detached magistrate. Coolidge's conviction for aggravated murder was reversed.

In some courtrooms across the country, you can get away with murder:

● In Utah, Gregory Fatzinger, who pleaded guilty to killing his girl friend's daughter, was placed on two years' probation and ordered to spend a year in a halfway house.

● In Colorado, Denver District Judge Alvin Lichtenstein sentenced Clarence Burns to two years of work release in the Denver County Jail after Burns killed his wife by shooting her five times in the face at close range.

● In Texas, State District Judge Miron Love sentenced Mark Pearson to 10 years' probation and a $500·fine for killing his father by shooting him six times. Judge Love said this was a case in which going to prison would be improper punishment.

Everyone who loves the Constitution and supports a sound criminal justice system owes it to the country to work for a system in which angry citizens will not feel compelled to take justice into their own hands.

We should, for example, direct Congress to undertake an exhaustive review of the 120 federal statutes which authorize the payment of mandatory or discretionary legal fees. Many of the categories in which awards are presently allowed should be eliminated.

For those areas in which Congress feels the fees should still be awarded, attorneys should be limited to $53 an hour, comparable to that paid senior government attorneys. In *no* case should an unsuccessful litigant be awarded attorney's fees.

As for the American Bar Association, it must decide if it wants to become again a "professional" organization concerned with the betterment of the legal profession, or if it wishes to continue as part and parcel of the modern liberal movement. If it chooses to continue as part of the liberal movement, concerned attorneys should think about establishing a populist-conservative professional alternative to the ABA.

The most basic step in reforming the legal system is to subject the system to the same intense scrutiny Americans bring to bear on legislators and other elected officials.

Professor Jules Gerard of Washington University in St. Louis has argued that there is no effective check on judicial excesses because judges enjoy lifetime tenure. Professor Gerard has noted that "Lifetime tenure lies at the heart of the misbehavior of federal judges . . . abolishing lifetime tenure is . . . the *sine qua non* of an effective system of ending judicial abuses of any variety.''

Professor Gerard has recommended a federal judicial system under which all federal judges would stand for popular reconfirmation every few years.

The federal system of lifetime tenure is not the rule when it comes to state judicial terms. Only four states—Massachusetts, New Hampshire, New Jersey and Rhode Island—give their judges lifetime tenure.

Federal judges have enjoyed lifetime tenure for some two centuries, and for many years, that system worked well. The rise of the highly centralized and powerful federal government, however, has brought dramatic increase in judicial power, with judges, particularly federal judges, no longer merely interpreting the law, but making the law.

Other things, short of abolition of life tenure, can be done by citizens as effective checks on activist courts.

One very innovative approach is the Washington Legal Foundation's ''Court Watch Project,'' designed to promote public scrutiny and accountability of prosecutors, judges and parole boards who are too lenient with criminals at the expense of crime victims and the law-abiding public.

The Foundation frequently receives reports either by telephone call or letter, often accompanied by newspaper articles about criminal cases which seem to have been decided without due regard to the public interest. By mid-1983, WLF had looked into some 500 judges at the state, local and federal level. Most were found to be simply doing their job, but in some cases, WLF initiated formal disciplinary review proceedings before state judicial conduct commissions and assisted in initiating others. Copies of the *Court Watch Manual* may be obtained by writing to the Washington Legal Foundation, Publications Department, 1612 K Street, N.W., Washington, D.C. 20006.

Perhaps the best-known populist remedy for judicial activism is withdrawal of jurisdiction over certain legal questions. This power is specifically granted to the Congress by Article III, Section 2 of the Constitution, which grants federal court jurisdictions with such exceptions and under such regulations as Congress will deem appropriate.

In October, 1982, Senator John East (R-N.C.) introduced the Judicial Reform Act, a comprehensive proposal designed to attack the problem of judicial activism at its core: the doctrine of incorporation under which federal courts have undermined or destroyed the framer's brilliant system of federalism.

The Judicial Reform Act would restore the intent of the Bill of Rights by removing from federal court jurisdiction those cases in which individuals claim a *state* abridgment of a right secured by the Bill of Rights. Unfortunately, a proposal as wise as Senator East's will not secure Congressional passage in the near future.

I have been critical of the Reagan Administration when I believe it has deviated from populist principles and sound political strategies. It is only fair, then, to point to the President's accomplishments in at least one area: improvement in criminal justice.

Since Ronald Reagan took office, there are some signs we may finally be turning the corner in the fight against crime. In August, 1983, the new *FBI Crime Statistics Report* showed a 3 percent drop in the overall serious crime rate. The staggering total of 12.9 million offenses committed during 1982 was, however, an astounding 47 percent higher than the total number of offenses committed only a decade ago. Even encouraging statistics can hide discouraging realities: despite improvements at the national level, in such places as New York City, crime in the elementary schools increased 11 percent between the 1981-82 and 1982-83 school years. Similar data emerges during detailed examination of the crime figures of the FBI and local jurisdictions.

It is clear that the President, with the help of important allies on Capitol Hill and in various organizations in the populist-conservative coalition, wants to move in the right direction on crime. On March 16, 1983, the President sent the Congress *The Comprehensive Crime Control Act of 1983*, a major reform package consisting of 16 separate titles which, if enacted, could constitute the most enduring legacy of the Reagan presidency.

Now, the Reagan anti-crime package was not perfect. Nevertheless, the overall package represented one of the rare occasions when this administration prepared a major initiative in consultation with its allies in the populist-conservative movement.

Everyone recognized that portions of the bill would be sacrificed in the legislative process. The final package approved by the Senate Judiciary Committee included only these elements: 1) uniform sentencing and the elimination of parole, 2) making "dangerousness" a factor in the determination of bail, 3) revising the insanity defense to place the burden of proving insanity on the defense and 4) transferring surplus federal property to state and local communities for use as jail space.

The revised package was virtually certain to pass the Senate in the fall of 1983, but its fate in the House of Representatives was much less certain. Attorney General William French Smith has described the House as the "one obstacle in the way of criminal justice reform."

Even if the administration package should secure House approval, much will remain to be done. Fortunately, a model exists for a permanent populist-conservative coalition on judicial reform and criminal justice issues.

The model for concerned Americans is the Kingston Coalition, which has operated successfully in Washington since 1972. The Kingston group is an informal weekly meeting of key activists and leaders from 30 or 40 organizations within the populist-conservative movement. The purpose of the meeting is to share information and promote action to achieve common goals. Action can consist of letter writing campaigns, meetings with key Congressional staffers or Members of Congress, communications to members in the various organizations, and a wide variety of other activities.

Frank Carrington—a veteran litigator for the rights of crime victims—has encouraged formation of a coalition on criminal justice issues. Patrick B. McGuigan, a sparkplug of activities in this area, has called for creation of a sort of "crime Kingston" meeting of populist-conservative and other organizations genuinely interested in restoring balance to the American legal system as whole, and the criminal justice system in particular. Dan Popeo of the Washington Legal Foundation has also been a leader in these efforts.

Such efforts should not be limited to the federal level. Citizens should form formal and informal working groups in their own communities, as needed, and make plans to support the efforts beginning at the national level.

What we need to do is educate ourselves so that we can scrutinize the courts and examine the work of judges fairly yet forcefully, with the same commitment we bring to examinations of Congressional voting records.

We should look for alternatives to lifetime tenure and develop specific programs such as "Court Watch" to focus popular attention on judicial excesses. We also need to offer general reform principles and proposals for the consideration of all Americans. Because the criminal justice system in particular needs substantial revision, concerned citizens must take the lead in reform. Finally, throughout the country populists should join with their fellow citizens in formal and informal coalitions to support meaningful, substantive and positive judicial reform.

8 / Big Media

The First Amendment to the Constitution guarantees a free press. But the Big Media are using this freedom to turn the nation's news media into a platform for their ultra-liberal, anti-populist philosophy.

Everywhere you look, on TV, in newspapers and magazines, you see:

- Extramarital sex glorified and marriage mocked.

- Bad news headlined and good news buried.

- Radicals and leftists featured and populists and conservatives ignored.

- Big cities glorified and small towns put down.

Why is what is good and true and decent about America reported poorly or not at all? Because the Big Media dominate the press to a degree never imagined by our Founding Fathers.

Consider:

The New York Times and *The Washington Post* are the two most influential newspapers in America. They are read every morning by national opinion leaders and other members of the media. ABC, CBS and NBC dominate television news. Two wire services, United Press International and Associated Press, provide most of the national and international news to the bulk of the nation's newspapers and broadcast outlets.

Selectivity is the weapon most often used by the Big Media against populists and Christians. Christian writers Francis and Franky Schaefer have sold hundreds of thousands of copies of their books but their books almost never appear on the *New York Times* Best Seller List and are seldom reviewed.

Pro-life demonstrations receive little coverage while pro-abortion demonstrations tend to receive major coverage. The Big Media elite make sure people, ideas and books they like receive wide public notice while people, ideas and books they don't like receive very little notice at all.

You know the news is slanted when you see conservatives referred to as "ultra-conservative," "far right," "ultra right," or "right wing" while liberals are rarely characterized as "ultra liberal," "radical," "left wing," or "leftist."

The leaders of anti-communist countries are referred to as "dictators" while Communist dictators like Castro and Andropov are referred to by their official title. Communist-supported revolutions are generally described as "civil wars."

Sometimes people are castigated for quotes they never made. CBS correspondent Lem Tucker in a broadcast on Oct. 13, 1981, said of Thomas Sowell, senior fellow at Hoover Institution, that his viewpoint "seems to place him in a school that believes that maybe most blacks are genetically inferior to whites." Sowell, who is black, had been arguing the exact opposite for 10 years in books, newspapers, magazines and numerous lectures.

The arrogance of the Big Media elite is unlimited (and often turns ugly).

Jesse Helms, the always polite and even courtly Senator from North Carolina, was described by the *Washington Post* as "the patron saint of the ultra right." Reference was made to Senator Helms' "stompin', trompin, ultra-right action."

Bryant Gumbel of NBC's "Today" complains that America has "a damn actor in the White House."

Seymour Hersh, then of the *New York Times*, said about the mass media: "Guess who is the final arbiter of national security in this democracy. We are."

Walter Cronkite told a convention of fellow journalists: "I don't think it is any of our business what the moral, political, social, or economic effect of our reporting is."

Tom Wicker, *New York Times* columnist, says, "What the press in America needs is less inhibition, not more restraint."

During the Vietnam war, a *Washington Post* writer referred to Bob Hope as "Bob (Let the Soldier Boys Die Laughing) Hope."

Sam Donaldson of ABC insists: "The record shows that not since about 1963, when Nikita Khrushchev, in a party-congress speech, made reference to world-wide Soviet hegemony, have they openly preached domination."

Who are these Big Media elite?

David Halberstam, former *New York Times* reporter and author of *The Powers That Be*, said of some of his colleagues: Phil Graham, publisher of *The Washington Post* until his death, was "very far left of center (in the 1930s) . . . and he used his paper accordingly."

Sander Vanocur, reporter for NBC and CBS: "Vanocur was regarded as a Kennedy man."

Carl Bernstein, of Watergate fame: "He was the child of left-wing parents, people of the thirties, New Dealers who had moved further left with the force of events."

It is even more revealing when the Big Media elite talk about themselves and their views of our country.

Tom Wicker, *New York Times* columnist, calls himself "a Southern liberal."

Walter Cronkite on television newsmen in general: "Well, certainly liberal, and possibly left of center as well . . . I think most newspapermen by definition have to be liberal; if they're not liberal, by my definition of it, then they can hardly be good newspapermen."

Geraldo Rivera of ABC about himself: "Remember that I'm coming from a radical background . . . I was politically far out."

Howard K. Smith, formerly of ABC, said his compatriots have a "strong leftward bias . . . Our liberal friends have become dogmatic. . . ."

Lowell Thomas, the late famous commentator: "I have spent my life in the communications world and I have discovered that perhaps 95 percent of all those involved, reporters, editors, and so on, are definitely to the left."

Katharine Graham, chairman of *The Washington Post*: "There is some validity in the allegation that we tend to draw our reporters from a common, narrow base. One of our staff members put it this way in a memo: 'Inevitably, the *Post* reflects the background biases of the people who put it out. We are for the most part a collection of Easterners . . . generally liberal.'"

David Levine, cartoonist for *The New York Review of Books* and *Esquire* in the 1960s: "I'm a socialist, so the concept of capitalist dogs in drawings can fit my partisan point of view."

Pete Hamill, New York columnist, said Richard Nixon was inhuman and "the single most aggressive purveyor of violence in the world." Lyle Deniston, *Baltimore Sun* reporter, said he saw no problem with stealing documents for publication even if it meant breaking and entering.

Newsweek magazine has argued that churches should accept homosexuality as part of God's plan of creation, implying that the traditional view of homosexuality as immoral should be rejected as old-fashioned.

What the Big Media elite say of themselves has been confirmed by academic research. George Washington University Professor S. Robert Lichter and Stanley Rothman, Professor at Smith College, interviewed 240 journalists and broadcasters and came up with this profile of the Big Media elite:

- Predominantly white males.

- 40 percent came from New York, New Jersey, Pennsylvania.

- Only 20 percent had fathers in blue collar or low status white collar jobs.

- 75 percent agreed with the statement that the West had not been helpful to Third World countries (despite $260 billion in foreign aid).

- 56 percent said the U.S. exploits Third World countries and is the cause of their poverty.

- 66 percent believed government should be in the business of redistributing income.

- 86 percent said they seldom if ever attend religious services.

- 91 percent voted for Lyndon Johnson in 1964, 87 percent voted for Hubert Humphrey in 1968, 81 percent voted for George McGovern in 1972, and 81 percent voted for Carter in 1976.

- 75 percent do not think that homosexuality is wrong.

- 85 percent uphold the right of homosexuals to teach in public schools.

- 54 percent do not regard adultery as wrong.

- Only 15 percent strongly agree that extramarital affairs are immoral.

Sometimes they go too far.

General William C. Westmoreland, who commanded our armed forces in Vietnam, was strongly criticized by CBS in a 90-minute documentary which alleged that he deliberately withheld intelligence information about enemy strength in Vietnam.

So flagrant was the slanting in this piece that *TV Guide* did an exposé and General Westmoreland has filed a $120 million slander suit.

Here are more examples of how the Big Media elite slant and make the news as they see fit:

Phyllis Schlafly, who led the successful fight against the ERA, was not invited to appear before the National Press Club in Washington until a year after the ERA had been defeated. For the almost ten years it was alive, those who supported the ERA were frequently provided the platform.

Barbara Honegger, a feminist with a minor post in the Justice Department, was made a major media celebrity when she quit with a blast at President Reagan for allegedly not doing enough for women. But when Dr. Bernard Nathanson, a prominent leader in the move to legalize abortion, changed sides and published a book, *Aborting America,* in which he explained why he thought abortion was a grave mistake, he was ignored by the media.

CBS challenged a statement by President Reagan that the Soviet ship, Alexander Ulyanov, was carrying military cargo to Nicaragua. CBS showed video tape of the ship and pointed out that no military cargo was visible. What they did not tell viewers, however, was they had purchased the tape from Communist Cuban film crews.

The leftist bias of the Big Media elite plays havoc in America's efforts to defend anti-communist governments from communist assaults. Inevitably the anti-communists are pictured as ''dictators'' while the communists are shown as ''reformers.''

Karen DeYoung, who covered the Sandinista revolution for *The Washington Post*, and is now that paper's foreign editor, never informed her readers that Sandinista leaders Tomas Borge, Daniel and Humberto Ortega, and Sergio Ramirez were hard-core Communists.

DeYoung has made no secret of where she stands politically. In a lecture at the Marxist-oriented Institute for Policy Studies, she said: "Most journalists now, most Western journalists at least, are very eager to seek out guerrilla groups, leftist groups, because you assume they must be the good guys."

Entertainment as Propaganda

Into every American home, television pours messages completely at odds with Judeo-Christian morality.

Television, like the print media, reflects the bias of the people who produce it. It is, for example, overwhelmingly anti-business, large or small.

A study by the Media Institute of over 200 prime time entertainment episodes from the 1979-80 season, found that two out of three businessmen on TV were portrayed as foolish, greedy or evil. In addition it found that:

● Over 50 percent of all corporate chiefs portrayed on television commit illegal acts ranging from fraud to murder.

● 45 percent of all business activities on television are portrayed as illegal.

● Only 3 percent of the businessmen on TV engage in socially useful or economically productive behavior.

● Hard work is usually ridiculed on TV as "workaholism" which inevitably leads to strained personal relations.

But ridiculing all businessmen is only part of the story. Sex and violence are the mainstays of television entertainment. This constant dosage of violence and immorality is

having a deadly effect on the minds of our children.
For example:

• Soon after 28-year-old David Radnis watched the movie,
"The Deer Hunter," on TV in his Chicago area home, he
was dead—one of at least 20 viewers in the U.S. who shot
themselves imitating the show's Russian roulette scene.

• In November, 1982, NBC aired "Executioner's Song,"
based on the life of convicted killer Gary Gilmore. (Why
choose a criminal psychopath in the first place?). In Hamilton, Ala., 20-year-old Jeffrey Alan Cox watched the program. Afterwards Cox shot his 77-year-old grandfather four
times in the head (like a scene in the program) and then did
the same thing to his 72-year-old grandmother. Cox had no
criminal record. Family members and law enforcement officials said they believed the movie triggered Cox's actions.

A report issued in May, 1983, by the National Institute
of Mental Health cited a five-year study of 732 children
where "several kinds of aggression—conflicts with parents,
fighting, and delinquency—were all positively correlated
with the total amount of television viewing."
The report concluded: ". . . violence on television does
lead to aggressive behavior by children and teenagers who
watch the programs . . . television can no longer be considered as a casual part of daily life, as an electronic toy.
Research findings have long since destroyed the illusion that
television is merely innocuous entertainment."
There is no better example of hypocrisy in the TV industry
than the standard denial that television doesn't influence
behavior. If TV doesn't have a powerful influence on people
then why do the networks charge, and corporations pay,
hundreds of thousands of dollars for one 30 second commercial?
Television has also been cited for the drop in scores of

the Scholastic Aptitude Test. The decline from 478 to 424 on the verbal exam and from 502 to 466 in mathematics from 1960 to 1982 coincides with the time when television became nearly universal.

How much sex and violence are actually on television? During the spring of 1983, the Coalition for Better Television monitored over 1200 hours of television shows. The number of sex incidents per hour was 8.7; for violence, 10.8 per hour; and for profanity 7.3 per hour.

Martha Rountree, a broadcast pioneer, has cited a Harvard study which states that approximately 70 percent of TV prime time shows make reference to sex with prostitutes or between unmarried couples. She said another survey found that during a two-month period network evening programming had 1,126 references to sex, 2,087 acts of violence, 1,619 suggestive remarks or uses of foul language, and 426 references to extramarital sex.

The responsibility for this mind pollution rests with the Big Media elite. But they show no sign of conscience about what they are doing to the minds and souls of the American people, especially our children. TV executives claim they are only doing their jobs by pursuing dollars and rating points. But in fact, they have sold their souls to the almighty dollar and are defiling their own country and fellow countrymen.

Researchers Lichter and Rothman also studied 104 creative people in TV. Like their counterparts in the print media, they are far different in their lifestyle and philosophy than the average American.

● 73 percent are from either California or the Boston-Washington corridor.

● 82 percent grew up in metropolitan areas.

● Only 15 percent come from blue collar backgrounds.

● 25 percent earn in excess of $500,000 a year and 63

percent report earnings in excess of $200,000.

● 93 percent say they seldom or never attend religious services.

● 75 percent describe themselves left of center.

● 97 percent believe in abortion on demand.

● 80 percent do not regard homosexual relations as wrong.

● 51 percent refuse to condemn adultery as wrong.

● 62 percent disagree that there is too much sex on TV.

● 66 percent believe TV entertainment should be a force for social reform.

This last point is all important. It means that the Big Media elite who determine much of our TV entertainment, believe they have the right to persuade us and our children to adopt their values.

Ben Stein, in his book, *The View from Sunset Boulevard*, studied script writers and found that their lifestyles generally matched the product of their typewriters, reflecting hedonism, immorality, and a use of drugs.

But the American people are catching on to the Big Media elite. Daniel Schorr, senior correspondent for Cable Network News, and formerly with CBS, wrote in the *Washington Post* in June, 1983: "One of the things that is changing is that the public no longer regards the press as its defender against the Establishment—but as the Establishment—as a big business less concerned with rights than with ratings."

The American people are also becoming more and more aware of the left-wing bias of the Big Media elite. They're learning that:

New York Times columnist Tom Wicker in 1983 spoke to veterans of the Abraham Lincoln Brigade, a well-known Communist front.

The Institute for Policy Studies, a pro-Marxist Washington think tank, is frequent host to media speakers. Its own people are frequent writers in national magazines and newspapers.

Among those who have spoken at the pro-Marxist IPS schools are: Karen DeYoung, *Washington Post* foreign editor; Frank Mankiewicz, former president of National Public Radio; Scott Armstrong, *Washington Post* investigative reporter; Peter Osnos, London correspondent for *The Washington Post*; John Dinges, *Washington Post*; Brian Ross and Jim Polk, NBC News; Les Whitten of Jack Anderson's staff; the late Jerry Landauer, *Wall Street Journal*; David Burnham, *New York Times*; and Charlene Hunter-Gault of the MacNeil-Lehrer public television program.

Many Big Media elitists have been in and out of government and partisan politics.

Frank Mankiewicz was in charge of press for George McGovern's 1972 presidential race.

Andrew Glass, Washington bureau chief of Cox Newspapers, is a former aide to liberal Republican Sen. Charles Percy, of Illinois.

Bill Moyers of CBS News was one of Lyndon Johnson's closest aides and advisers.

David Burke, vice president of ABC News, was a former aide to New York Governor Hugh Carey and Senator Edward Kennedy.

Leslie Gelb, *New York Times* reporter, was in the Carter State Department.

Tom Johnson, publisher of the *Los Angeles Times,* was an LBJ White House aide.

Seymour Hersh, author of an expose of Henry Kissinger and an investigative reporter who broke the story on My Lai, was press secretary for Senator Eugene McCarthy's presidential campaign.

Edwin Guthman, editor of the *Philadelphia Inquirer*'s editorial page, was an aide to Attorney General Robert Kennedy.

Jody Powell, ABC commentator and newspaper columnist, was Press Secretary to President Jimmy Carter.

Of the media stars who have been in and out of government only a tiny fraction worked with non-liberal politicians. CBS morning News co-anchor Diane Sawyer and columnists Pat Buchanan and William Safire all worked for Richard Nixon.

TV networks also refuse to sell advertising time to presidential candidates until shortly before the primaries, giving an advantage to their choices, to whom they give favorable "news coverage."

Nor will the TV networks accept issue advertising. People who want to speak out on abortion, communism, tax relief, bail-out of the big banks, or any other public issue are shut out by the networks which refuse to accept such advertising on the grounds that it is "controversial."

Public television and public radio are even farther left. The Corporation for Public Broadcasting spends taxpayers' money on public television and public radio. The bulk of its programming is to the left of even American liberals. Public TV broadcast a hatchet job on the CIA, "On Company Business," based on allegations of Philip Agee, who owned a percentage of the film. Agee, a former CIA agent, has said in public: "I aspire to be a communist and a revolutionary." None of Agee's ideological background was given to the Public TV viewers.

Public radio relies heavily on socialist and pro-Marxist commentators to "analyze" events. They have used, for example, Professor Richard R. Fagen of Stanford to analyze President Reagan's Central American policies. Fagen has a long history of support for Castro and the Sandinista regime in Nicaragua.

The CPB has given at least $1.6 million to a Marxist radio network, Radio Pacifica, which includes WPFW in Washington, D.C. This station has described U.S. efforts to save El Salvador from a communist takeover as "indiscriminate, genocidal oppression equal to that of the Nazis." Radio Pacifica, to which CPB gives our tax dollars, described the neutron bomb as a weapon to be used against the blacks of the United States.

Perhaps the most serious and dangerous impact of the Big Media is on our children.

When you realize that children spend an average of 25 hours a week with television, then you can understand why so many children abandon Judeo-Christian values and patriotism for the immoral, anti-freedom socialist values of the elitists.

Most U.S. daily newspapers make money from pornographers. Advertisements for X and XXX rated movies, including photos from the movies, are a routine part of all but a few daily newspapers. These same newspapers are within easy reach of children who, scanning the movie guides, can't help but see the graphic nature of such ads, including those pushing homosexual films.

The Big Media elite are responsible for:

- Sex on TV at all times of the day.

- XXX rated movie ads in family newspapers.

- Sex on the radio.

- Over 95 percent of all movies shown at local theaters featuring such themes as pre-marital sex, extra-marital sex and homosexual relationship.

- Christian life being made fun of.

- Violence glorified.

- Drugs presented as smart and fashionable.

Establishment groups make much of the danger of water pollution or air pollution. But a much greater danger is the moral pollution coming into our homes from TV and other Big Media.

A wise jurist once said that freedom of speech does not entitle someone to yell, ''Fire!'' in a crowded theater.

And the right to a free press does not entitle the Big Media to pour violence and filth and anti-Americanism into our homes and places of work.

It's time we let the Big Media know how out of step with the spirit of America they are.

Elite Country

An ancient Chinese Proverb says "one picture is worth ten thousand words."

In this book I've tried to describe how the elite establishment is messing up our lives, and who and what it is. This chapter follows that proverb's advice.

Some of the world's best political cartoonists have graphically described how we are victimized by the establishment and its elitist policies.

While the cartoons are humorous, the message to the elite establishment is clear—get off our backs.

"If he bolts, we got trouble."

"*We might make unwise international loans, Mr. Simpson, but we don't make unwise loans to individuals.*"

"Let's leave out 'No Taxation without Representation'! What congress would vote taxes without consulting the people?"

Reprinted by permission of Tribune Company Syndicate, Inc.

REAGAN'S PROBLEM IS THAT HE'S FORGOTTEN HIS ROOTS. HE'S BECOME ONE OF THE 'COUNTRY CLUB' SET.
(UM, DON'T FORGET MY GOLF SHOES, BENTLEY.)

TIP

"AND THIS IS THE HOUSE CLOAKROOM WHERE THE MEMBERS GATHER TO GO OVER LAST MINUTE STRATEGY BEFORE VOTING ON THE FLOOR....APPARENTLY, THEY'RE ON THEIR WAY TO VOTE ON THE PAY RAISE."

"I WENT OVER OUR FALL LINE-UP, J.R. IT'S FULL OF SIMPLE-MINDED STORY LINES, VIOLENCE AND SEXUAL INNUENDOS, IT SHOULD BE A GREAT SEASON!"

"NO, I'M NOT OVER-STAFFED.   I DO THE WORK AND
THE OTHERS KEEP THE RECORDS FOR THE GOVERNMENT."

Thanks to you, Lee is smiling again.

But others like him need your help.

□ I'd like to aid a needy corporation.
Enclosed is my gift of $____,000,000,000
Send to: CORPORATE AID SOCIETY
         ℅ U.S. TREASURY
         WASHINGTON, D.C.

Name ....
Address ....
City .... State .... Zip ......

MARGULIES ROTHCO

MARGULIES   ROTHCO CARTOONS

83-29E35

JOHN BRANCH
Courtesy San Antonio Express-News

What better place to cut?

9 / From the Horse's Mouth

One of the principal methods used by the establishment to maintain its power is to establish certain opinions as legitimate and others as foolish. For example, that investment of Federal tax dollars in various programs, from education to highway construction, would not lead to Federal control; the contrary opinion was considered foolish. During the debate over creation of the modern version of the income tax, the legitimate opinion was that the tax would never exceed two percent; the contrary opinion was considered foolish.

Today, when individuals voice opinions held by a majority of the people—such as cut taxes, cut spending, balance the budget, increase defense preparedness, reduce or end needless regulations—they are often attacked by the establishment elite. They are accused of being out of step, living in the Dark Ages, or being reactionary. At best, they are made to look silly. At worst, they are described as dangerous and obstructionist.

But the real story, one which rarely sees the light of day, is what the establishment thinks about America and her people. It is not the populists who are out of touch with reality, it is the establishment.

I have brought together statements by members of the establishment and their allies. Most of these people are considered liberal: the kind of liberal who pretends to speak for the people.

In fact, by their own statements, these establishment representatives show the contempt they feel towards the average American, and toward those values held dear by most working people. It is a contempt that goes beyond current political and social issues, to the very foundation of our nation and society.

It is clear that, if the establishment had absolute power, we would witness the loss of many, if not all, of the freedoms we take for granted: the American nation would become the plaything of the establishment elite; her people, their pawns.

These are the people who think *your* ideas and beliefs are foolish.

GOVERNMENT/POLITICAL

Walter Mondale:

"I'm very worried about US-Soviet relations. I cannot understand—it just baffles me—why the Soviets these last few years have behaved as they have. Maybe we have made some mistakes with them . . ."[1]

"The sickening truth is that this country is rapidly coming to resemble South Africa. Our native reserves and Bantustans are the inner city. And our apartheid is all the more disgusting for being insidious and unproclaimed."[2]

Richard Nixon is "the most miserable man ever to occupy any public office" in America.

[1]*Conservative Digest*, Jan., 1981.
[2]Arnold Beichman, *The Washington Times*, Feb. 28, 1983.

Jimmy Carter:

The government of El Salvador, under attack by Soviet-funded Communist revolutionaries, is "the most blood-thirsty in our hemisphere, perhaps in the world . . ."[3]

"Being confident of our own future, we are now free of that inordinate fear of Communism which once led us to embrace any dictator who joined us in that fear. I am glad that this is being changed."[4]

Frank Church, Former U.S. Senator (Idaho):

After a 1975 visit to Cuba, "I found his [Castro's] views to be reasonable, objective and surprisingly moderate."[5]

George McGovern:

"I'd be insulted if Castro lied."[6]

America's policies in Vietnam were "the most barbaric and inhumane since Adolph Hitler."

Ho Chi Minh is "the George Washington of his country."[7]

"I've never really gone along with this Cold War. I don't think the Russians are the traditional maniacs we make them out to be."[8]

"These people (conservative religious groups) have been getting away with dirty tactics in American politics for too long a time. I regard them as a menace to the American political process."[9]

" 'The Moral Majority' . . . 'The New Right' . . . 'The Right to Life Movement' . . . 'Pro Family' . . . Whatever name it's called, the Extreme Right is . . . posing an un-

---

[3]*The Washington Post*, Jul. 20, 1983.
[4]Speech at Notre Dame University, May 22, 1977.
[5]Patrick J. Buchanan, *Human Events*, Sept. 20, 1980.
[6]*National Review*, Jul. 7, 1978.
[7]Jeffrey Hart, *The Washington Times*, Jun. 27, 1983.
[8]*Human Events*, Jun. 19, 1982.
[9]*U.S. News and World Report*, Nov. 17, 1980.

precedented threat to individual rights . . . and individual liberties. It is seeking to subvert the Constitution itself.''[10]

California's 1978 Proposition 13 tax revolt was ''racist'' and ''unAmerican.''[11]

Sargent Shriver, George McGovern's 1972 Vice
Presidential running mate:

President Nixon is ''the greatest murderer in the world today.''

Henry Kissinger:

''You don't get reelected to the Presidency on a platform that admits you got behind. You talk instead about the great partnership for peace achieved in your term.''[12]

Ron Dellums, Member of Congress (Calif.):

''Fascism is the reality in this country, it's just not formalized.''[13]

The U.S. has got rich on the backs of ''slave labor.''[14]

''What is taking place in America today is genocide.''[15]

Anti-Communism is ''a scapegoat to cover racism and war.''[16]

''I have attempted to aid the Black Panthers whenever I could . . .'' the Panthers are ''the scapegoats of the '60s . . . the attack on the Panthers is tantamount to Fascism.''[17]

Charles Percy, U.S. Senator (Ill.):

America cannot afford ''the extravagance of simplistic dogmatism. We cannot wage holy wars of anticommunism

---

[10]American Civil Liberties Union fund raising letter signed by McGovern, Jan., 1981.

[11]Kenneth Roberts, *New Guard*, Summer 1983.

[12]*On Watch*, by Elmo Zumwalt, Times Books, New York, 1976.

[13]Francis J. McNamara, *Human Events*, Mar. 29, 1975.

[14]Ibid.

[15]Ibid.

[16]Ibid.

[17]Ibid.

. . . Let us deal with the real world, not with a world of make believe in which all communists are equally villainous and America is presumed to be 99 and 44/100 percent pure.''[18]

John Dingell, Member of Congress (Mich.):

Competition from ''the little yellow people'' is hurting the domestic automobile industry.[19]

Hamilton Jordan, White House Chief of Staff, Carter Administration:

''Carter will really go on gun control and really be tough. We're going to get those bastards (anti-gun control group).''[20]

Victor Utgoff, Adviser, Strategic Arms Limitation, National Security Council, Carter Administration:

''Even if the U.S could obtain strategic superiority it would not be desirable because I suspect we would occasionally use it as a way of throwing our weight around in some very risky ways . . . It is in the U.S. interest to allow the few remaining areas of strategic advantage to fade away.''[21]

John Anderson, Independent Presidential Candidate, 1980:

''The stakes are so high and our efforts to win an arms race so unavailing that I would be willing to accept some identifiable risks in order to halt the arms race.''[22]

Ramsey Clark, U.S. Attorney General, Johnson Administration:

''. . . the American Government attaches no importance to the lives of the (American hostages in Iran) but is using

---

[18]Michigan Republican Convention, Feb., 1967.
[19]*The New Right Report*, May 28, 1982.
[20]*The New York Times*, Dec. 10, 1976.
[21]M. Stanton Evans, *Human Events*, Jun. 30, 1979.
[22]*The News American*, Baltimore, Mar. 24, 1983.

them in its own interest in order to achieve its colonialist aims . . .'' The failed U.S. rescue mission was "a lawless military expedition, an assault on the sovereign territory of Iran."[23]

Birch Bayh, Former U.S. Senator (Ind.):

"I don't intend to sit still and let it (conservative success in defeating him and other liberals in 1980) happen in the tradition of Nazi Germany where no one spoke out when it started."[24]

Marion Barry, Mayor of Washington, D.C.:

"You should let people know you will support your friends and punish your enemies." (Addressing Gay and Lesbian Pride Day, 1981)[25]

Thomas P. "Tip" O'Neill:

"I think that he (President Reagan) has very, very selfish people around him, very selfish people around him . . ."[26]
". . . the John Birchers are now in control of the Republican Party."[27]

Bella Abzug, Former Member of Congress (N.Y.):

America is "imperialistic . . . power mad . . . a vehicle for murder and oppression."

Alan Cranston, U.S. Senator (Calif.):

"We have never made—never—an arms control effort that is sufficiently creative, constructive, determined and *fair to the Soviet Union* (italics added)."[28]

[23]Editorial, *Human Events*, June 21, 1980.
[24]United Press International, Nov. 7, 1980.
[25]*The Washington Post*, Jun. 22, 1981.
[26]*Issues and Answers*, ABC-TV, Jul., 1980.
[27]Associated Press, Jul. 31, 1980.
[28]George Will, *The Washington Post*, Feb. 6, 1983.

J. William Fulbright, Former U.S. Senator (Ark.):

The political movement backing Barry Goldwater for President in 1964 was "the closest thing in American politics to Russian Stalinism."[29]

The uprising in El Salvador is an "indigenous revolution" and the United States may be supporting the wrong side.[30]

Bill Moyers, Former White House Press Secretary, Johnson Administration, now a CBS Commentator:

I "hung the nuclear noose around Goldwater and finished him off."[31]

Edward Kennedy, U.S. Senator (Mass.):

"The new American Ambassador to the United Nations (Jeanne Kirkpatrick) openly encourages dictators and juntas to be 'moderately repressive'."[32]

Alvin Holmes, State Representative (Ala.):

"We're in a hell of a fix. We've got to choose between Hitler (Wallace) and Mussolini (Folmer). But at least Hitler is a Democrat. So we're selecting the lesser of two evils."[33]

Edmund "Pat" Brown, Then-Governor (Calif.):

Following Barry Goldwater's nomination as the 1964 Republican presidential candidate, he said, "I smell the stench of Nazism. I hear the march of storm troopers."[34]

---

[29]*New Guard,* the magazine of Young Americans For Freedom, Summer 1983.

[30]United Press International, Mar. 16, 1982.

[31]*It Didn't Start With Watergate,* by Victor Lasky, The Dial Press, 1977.

[32]Fund raising letter, Fund for a Democratic Majority, 1981.

[33]*The Washington Post,* Oct. 28, 1982.

[34]*New York Times,* Aug. 8, 1964.

Sam Brown, Director of ACTION, Carter
                Administration:

"Politics is a struggle to redistribute power and wealth.
That's what I'm all about."[35]

Ann Lewis, Political Director, Democratic National
                Committee:

"Gay rights is no longer a debatable issue within the
Democratic Party."[36]

The National Committee for an Effective Congress:

"While we're watching them (Presidential candidates
Reagan, Anderson, Carter) . . . somebody else is *stealing*
Congress (Thurmond, Helms, Dole, Baker) . . . don't let
the Right Wing *steal* Congress."[37]

Charles T. Manatt, Chairman, Democratic National
                Committee:

"I consider formation of the national association (of Gay
and Lesbian Democratic Clubs) an important step . . . I
know that you share my pride (in) the commitment of this
party to end any discrimination based on sexual orientation."[38]

MEDIA

Flora Lewis, Columnist, *New York Times,* Paris Bureau:

"There are certain profound similarities in the theses
advanced by the Red Guards who rampaged through China
a few years ago in the name of Mao, the Ayatollah Khom-

---

[35]*Conservative Digest,* Jun., 1978.
[36]Patrick Buchanan, *The Washington Times*, Aug. 1, 1983.
[37]Fund raising letter, Sept., 1980.
[38]Letter to Tom Chorlton, National Association of Gay and Lesbian Democratic Clubs, Aug. 30, 1982.

eini's wild-eyed Islamic principles, the orthodox militants of Israel and the Americans who call themselves the Moral Majority."[39]

Herbert Matthews, Former foreign correspondent, *New York Times*:

"(Castro has) strong ideas of liberty, democracy, social justice, the need to restore the Constitution, to hold elections . . . 'we are fighting for a democratic Cuba and an end to dictatorship, (Castro says).' "[40]

Seymour Hersh, Former reporter, *New York Times*:

"His character (Ho Chi Minh) was certainly sterling."[41]
"Guess who is the final arbiter of national security in this democracy. We are."

Walter Cronkite:

"I don't think it is any of our business what the moral, political, social or economic effect of our reporting is."
"There are always groups in Washington expressing views of alarm over the state of our defenses. We (CBS Evening News) don't carry those stories. The story is that there are those who want to cut defense spending."[42]

CIVIL RIGHTS

Rev. Andrew Young, Then Ambassador to the U.N., Carter Administration:

There are "hundreds, perhaps thousands, of political prisoners in the United States."[43]

---

[39]*The New York Times*, Nov. 28, 1980.
[40]*The New York Times*, Feb. 24, 1957.
[41]John D. Lofton Jr., *The Washington Times*, Aug. 31, 1983.
[42]Patrick Buchanan, *Conservative Digest*, April, 1977.
[43]Allan H. Ryskind, *Human Events*, Feb. 21, 1981.

"I don't see any difference in the so-called due process of Florida (accorded convicted murderer John Spenkelink) and the so-called due process of Khomeini."[44]

"Communism has never been a threat to me."[45]

If Reagan wins, "black folks will catch hell for the rest of this century."[46]

States rights "Looks like a code word to me that it's going to be all right to kill niggers . . ."[47]

(Jimmy Carter: Andrew Young, is a "national treasure," a "Third World Hero," "finest elected official" and "best man" I have ever known.)[48]

Coretta Scott King:

"I am scared that if Ronald Reagan gets into office, we are going to see more of the Ku Klux Klan and a resurgence of the Nazi Party."[49]

". . . the Klan would be quite comfortable" with Ronald Reagan.[50]

Roy Wilkins, Former President, NAACP:

"If Barry Goldwater is President, it could lead to a police state."[51]

Roger Baldwin, Founder, ACLU:

"I am for socialism, disarmament and ultimately for abolishing the state as an instrument of violence and compulsion. I seek social ownership of property, the abolition of the

[44]John D. Lofton, Jr., *Human Events*, Jul. 7, 1979.

[45]*Conservative Digest*, Apr.,1980.

[46]Patrick J. Buchanan, *National Comment*, May, 1981.

[47]Ibid.

[48]Carl Gershman, *Commentary*, Aug., 1978.

[49]Associated Press, Nov. 3, 1980.

[50]Patrick J. Buchanan, *National Comment*, May, 1981.

[51]*What Happened To Goldwater?*, by Steven Shadegg; Holt, Rinehart and Winston, 1965.

propertied class and sole control by those who produce wealth. Communism is the goal."[52]

Coleman Young, Mayor, Detroit, Mich.:

"Ronald Reagan is crazy, trigger-happy and dangerous . . . the Prune Face of the West."[53]

Aaron Henry, President, Mississippi NAACP:

To America's blacks, Ronald Reagan's "name is anathema, like Hitler's"[54]

Clarence Mitchell, Former Director, Washington D.C., NAACP:

"The Reagan victory is a calamity for civil rights. It was made possible by a revival of latent racism in our society."[55]

Dorothy Gilliam, Staff Columnist, *The Washington Post*:

"A key to the current pessimism of blacks is the time at which Ronald Reagan is ascending power. The Ku Klux Klan is coming out of the closet, there are vicious, random murders of black children and adults."[56]

Rev. Jesse Jackson, Civil Rights Activist:

Reagan's campaign appeal "was to the very base, racist instincts of white people."[57]

Julian Bond, State Senator (Georgia):

On the conservative movement in America: ". . . if you listen carefully, you can hear the distant drums of soldiers marching to the familiar tune of 'the pure race' . . . Con-

---

[52]Phyllis Schlafly, *The Washington Post*, Jul. 14, 1982.
[53]Patrick J. Buchanan, *National Comment*, May, 1981.
[54]Ibid.
[55]*The Sun*, Baltimore, Nov. 9, 1980.
[56]*The Washington Post*, Nov. 8, 1980.
[57]United Press International, Nov. 8, 1980.

servative political leaders backed by 'Moral Majority' preachers have called for a return to the darker days of our past.''[58]

Rev. Martin Luther King:

''We have been in a reform movement . . . but we moved into a new era, which must be an era of revolution.''[59]

''America is deeply racist and its democracy is flawed both economically and socially . . . radical reconstruction of society itself is the real issue to be faced.''[60]

''The whole structure of American life must be changed.''[61]

UNION OFFICERS

Kenneth Blaylock, President, American Federation of Government Employees:

''Instead of picking candidates who offer constructive solutions to problems, American voters seemed to fall prey to the strident zealots who dominated the entire campaign . . .''[62]

Jim Kerns, President, Idaho State AFL-CIO:

Labor's problems in the Idaho legislature will continue ''unless we have a series of accidents and kill a bunch of these'' pro-right to work legislators.[63]

George Meany, Late President, AFL-CIO:

After Barry Goldwater's nomination as the Republican candidate for President, he said, there is ''a parallel between

---

[58]In a letter to potential members of Klanwatch, a project of The Southern Poverty Law Center, 1980.

[59]Charles D. Brennan, former FBI assistant director, *Conservative Digest*, Sept., 1983.

[60]Ibid.

[61]Ibid.

[62]Mike Causey, *The Washington Post*, Nov. 9, 1980.

[63]*National Right to Work Newsletter*, Jun. 30, 1983.

Senator Barry Goldwater and Adolph Hitler.''[64]

William Winpisinger, Vice President, AFL-CIO:

Doctors are ''sons of bitches'' who are ''out of step with all the rest of us.''[65]

The Republican Party is the ''neutron bomb'' whose philosophy is ''kill all the poor people and let the real estate live on.''[66]

The US Defense Department's effort to arm us is ''that f---ing Pentagon madness.''[67]

The oil industry is a ''Goddamn bunch of private profiteers'' that should be nationalized.[68]

Dolores Huerta, First Vice President, United Farm
Workers:

''Reagan hates Hispanics.''[69]

Lane Kirkland, President, AFL-CIO:

''If all else fails and people come to the conclusion that the only way they can get people's attention is to create turmoil in the streets, then I guess, perhaps, we have to go out and organize some turmoil in the streets if that's what it takes to convince people.''[70]

RELIGIOUS

Rev. M. William Howard, President National Council
of Churches:

''There is an unnerving similarity between Jerry Falwell and the Ayatollah Khomeini.''[71]

[64]*AFL-CIO News*, Aug. 8, 1964.
[65]John D. Lofton, Jr., *The Washington Times*, Aug. 19, 1983.
[66]Ibid.
[67]Ibid.
[68]Ibid.
[69]Patrick J. Buchanan, *National Comment*, May, 1981.
[70]*The New York Times*, Dec. 4, 1982.
[71]John Weisman, *TV Guide*, Washington Baltimore edition, Nov. 1, 1980.

Catholic Archbishop Raymond Hunthausen of Seattle:

The Trident submarine base in Washington state is "the Auschwitz of Puget Sound."[72]

Catholic Archbishop John Quinn of San Francisco:

Urged Catholic hospitals to refuse cooperation with U.S. civil defense planners.[73]

Catholic Bishop Deroy Mathiesen of Amarillo:

Asked employees of the nearby Pantex Company, which assembles all America's nuclear warheads, to consider leaving their jobs.[74]

Rev. Carl Flemister, Executive Minister, American Baptist Churches of Metropolitan New York:

"When you have a religious leader like Jerry Falwell saying we need more Christians in government, that's talking like the Ku Klux Klan."[75]

ENTERTAINMENT

Jane Fonda:

America is "a war machine" and "a murderer . . . barbaric."

"I would think that if you understood what Communism was, you would hope, you would pray on your knees that we would some day become Communists."[76]

---

[72]*Time*, Nov. 29, 1982.
[73]*The Economist*, Oct. 24, 1981.
[74]Ibid.
[75]*The New York Daily News*, Sept. 14, 1980.
[76]*Conservative Digest*, Apr., 1980.

Gore Vidal, Author:

"Marriage is breaking up, and it's a good thing. Much of the illness of our time comes from it . . ."[77]

Husbands and wives "who stray from the ideal" of fidelity waste their money going to psychiatrists and marriage counselors. "Better to buy a boy or girl and have sex for an hour. It would be much more relaxing and to the point."[78]

Edward Asner, Actor, Portrayed "Lou Grant" on *The Lou Grant Show*:

"A full-scale war is now raging in (El Salvador) . . . and every day the involvement of the United States Government escalates. Tragically, we're on the wrong side (in El Salvador) once again."[79]

(Reed Irvine: "A lot of criticism has been directed at Asner, some of it for his statement that if other people chose to live under communism, so be it. Mr. Asner would be hard pressed to name any country that had 'chosen' communism. The one thing that all communist countries have in common is their avoidance of free elections.")[80]

Leonard Bernstein, Composer-Conductor:

We must "rescue that much abused word patriotism from the clutching hands of America's bigots . . . It seems (to be) the private property of the most narrow minded group, of Klansmen, America Firsters, demogogic evangelists who are anti-black, anti Semitic, anti-labor, anti-abortionist, anti-gay rights, anti-civil liberties, and anti-human rights.

"If Ronald Reagan becomes president every one of these

---

[77]*Human Events*, May 1, 1982.
[78]Ibid.
[79]*The New York Times*, Feb. 20, 1982.
[80]*Accuracy in Media*, Mar. 18, 1982.

nightmarish figures are going to come riding in with him, high in the saddle.''[81]

FEMINISTS

The Document: A Declaration of Feminism:

''. . . the end of the institution of marriage is a necessary condition for the liberation of women. Therefore, it is important for us to encourage women to leave their husbands and not to live individually with men . . . we must work to destroy (marriage).''[82]

Dr. Mary Jo Bane, Associate Professor, Harvard University:

''. . . It's a dilemma. In order to raise children with equality, we must take them away from families and communally raise them.''[83]

Gloria Steinem, Editor, *Ms.* Magazine:

''By the year 2000 we will, I hope, raise our children to believe in human potential, not God . . .''[84]

''We no longer can depend on the electoral system. The street is the only place for our movement.''[85]

''The lawful and peaceful stage of our revolution may be over. It's up to the legislators. We can become radical, if they force us. If they continue to interfere with the ratification of the ERA, they will find every form of disobedience possible in every state of the country.''[86]

---

[81]United Press International, Oct. 19, 1980.
[82]Published by Karen Clark, Sandy Gerber, Nancy Lehmann, Susan Miller, and Helen Fullinger, 1971.
[83]*Tulsa World*, Aug. 21, 1977.
[84]*Saturday Review of Education*, Mar., 1973.
[85]*Human Events*, Feb. 25, 1978.
[86]M. Stanton Evans, *Human Events*, Jul. 22, 1978.

Betty Friedan, Founder, National Organization of
Women:

"No deity will save us, we must save ourselves. Promises
of immortal salvation or fear of eternal damnation are both
illusory and harmful."[87]

OTHERS

Dr. James Cheek, President, Howard University,
Washington, D.C.:

"In 26 years since waging a world war against the forces
of tyranny, fascism and genocide in Europe, we have become
a nation more tyrannical, more fascistic, and more capable
of genocide than was ever conceived or thought possible
two decades ago. We conquered Hitler, but we have come
to embrace Hitlerism."[88]

Ansel Adams, Environmentalist/Photographer:

"I hate Santa Barbara and, far worse, I hate Reagan."[89]

Thomas Theobald, Senior Vice President, Citibank:

(On the possible default on American loans to Poland):
"Who knows which political system works? The only test
we care about is, can they pay their bills?"[90]

David Rockefeller, Chairman of the Board, Chase
Manhattan Bank:

(On the question of loans to Marxist Angola): "I don't
think an international bank such as ours ought to try to set
itself as a judge about what kind of government a country

---

[87]As cosignator, "Humanist Manifesto II," Prometheus Books, 1973.
[88]Arnold Beichman, *The Washington Times,* Feb. 28, 1983.
[89]*Newsweek,* Apr. 4, 1983.
[90]*Conservative Digest,* October, 1982

wishes to have. We have found that we can deal with just about any kind of government, provided that they are orderly and responsible.''

10 / The Voices of Populism

More and more people are flocking to the populist banner. They are Republican and Democrat, Christian and Jew, black and white, male and female, young and old, people from the South, North, East, and West.

Some are attracted by populism's emphasis on the family, others by its Judeo-Christian heritage, still others by its belief in the can-do spirit of free enterprise. But all share a common faith in the people's ability to make their own decisions in their own way in their own time. They all reject the elitist notion that only Big Government and Big Business and Big Unions and Big whatever can do it better.

As these quotes from some of our nation's most distinguished citizens demonstrate, the New Populism is no longer an idea or a passing fancy. The New Populism is a movement ready to be a major force in American politics and American society.

"Today populism is the movement to restore the people's rights and prerogatives that our founding fathers had in mind in the first place."
　　　　—HON. WILLIAM ARMSTRONG, U.S. Senator (Colorado)

"Populism as I see it is an optimistic view of the people. It says they make better decisions about their own lives than would the most superbly trained elite, simply because they know more about their lives than anyone else.''

> —JEFF BELL, De Witt Wallace Fellow in Communications at American Enterprise Institute

''Populism remains a tradition in American politics because the people still live their lives apart from big government, big business, and big banks.

''The eighties should see the emergence of a 'new populism' composed of citizens from a wide philosophical, ethnic, and economic spectrum. This emergence is a result of the growing public awareness that these massive institutions have their own agenda and special interests which exclude the interests of the man on the street.''

> —NEAL BLAIR, President, Free The Eagle

''Populism is a strategy in the negative, a way of coming together to say no, and only by implication a political philosophy. For it is also a way of saying yes to the example of the American Revolution, of joining our neighbors in rebellion against a remote arrogant and arbitrary power which threatens to impose upon us some plan for the common good that is not indigenous or in keeping with what Patrick Henry called 'the genius of the people.' The stateman as populist speaks *for* an outraged 'we' and enjoins its members to go after a nefarious vimp. In so proceeding he avoids altogether the rhetoric of class or constituency—except where the meddling enemy is concerned.''

> —DR. M. E. BRADFORD, Professor of English and American Studies, University of Dallas/Vice President of the Philadelphia Society

''Rooted in Judeo-Christian values, the New Populism is a Fighting Faith—a traditionalist, nationalist, patriotic people's counter-revolution as much at war with the moral relativism and material decadence of the West, as it is with the monstrous tyrannies of the East.''

> —PATRICK J. BUCHANAN, Syndicated Columnist

"The great men who founded the United States didn't have straw between their teeth— but they were populist. Jefferson, Madison and Adams were all well-fixed, cultivated gentlemen. When Washington was sworn in as President, he was the wealthiest man in the United States. But all these men were of the party of the people. They believed that ordinary citizens really should shape the direction of government, and that our trust for its successful conduct, never very great in any event, should be the highest with them. Sadly, this view is in eclipse today.

"I don't know who America's wealthiest citizen is now. But I doubt that he has Washington's populist confidence. Too many of our leading citizens have had a failure of nerve. They really don't believe that we should put our trust in the people. In fact, if nothing else were known about a political opinion, except that it is popular, that would be a presumption against it in the eyes of the news media and the other well-fixed and presumably enlightened gentlemen and women who are trying to run the United States today."

> —JAMES DALE DAVIDSON, Chairman of the National Taxpayers Union.

"The strength of populism lies in the fact that it is far easier for the people to make wise decisions on issues than on the shifting promises and personalities of individuals.

"A proposition duly placed on the ballot by petition, can't change its mind after the polls are closed.

"Our nation was founded as a democratic republic but more and more today voters feel a sense of disillusion and helplessness. They sense that their vote just won't make a difference and that in our republic democracy is being slowly but surely replaced by bureaucracy. Thus we need now more than ever the remedy of the process of popular voter initiatives when legislators and the Congress ignore the will of the people."

> —EDWARD "CHIP" DENT, President, Americans for the National Voter Initiative Amendment

"What is the new populist movement that is sweeping the country? A combination of conservatives, libertarians and all others who share a mutual distrust of the powers of the monolithic federal government.

"The new populist believes in limiting the federal bureaucracy and maximizing individual freedom. They share the belief that the best way the federal government can help a man is to help that man help himself.

"By this, the new populist movement stands strong for letting each individual form his own destiny through the use of each individual's unique talents and initiatives.

"While some populists may disagree on various issues, their main goal is agreed on by all . . . limit the power of government and let freedom ring for everyone."

> —JOHN T. "TERRY" DOLAN, Chairman, National Conservative
> Political Action Committee (NCPAC)

"The populist movement in this country is held together by that strong moral fiber spun at the birth of this Nation. It speaks from the very soul of this country. It is what this country was and can be again."

> —DR. JERRY FALWELL, President, Moral Majority

"There is a natural antithesis between the rights of the common man, whether natural and God-given or civil rights granted by the Constitution, and the vested interests of those who possess political and/or economic power at any given moment. The new populists are not revolutionaries but those who understand that the strength of the nation is the strength and involvement of its constituent part, informed and motivated citizens. The U.S. Constitution and the Bill of Rights recognize this when they speak of 'the consent of the governed'."

> —FATHER CHARLES FIORE, O.P., Chairman, National Pro-Life
> Political Action Committee

"Populist policy is America's only weapon against gradual Western surrender and withdrawal and our best weapon against a tyrannical empire whose greatest weakness is its own failure to meet the aspiration of its own people.''

—GREG FOSSEDAL, Staff Writer, *The Wall Street Journal*

''The new populism is the most promising force in American life, not only for an Establishment culture still wallowing in a secular hedonist swamp, but also for our national economy. The creation of value necessarily requires a spirit of discipline and sacrifice that a secular liberal society can find no way to either justify or evoke. And the value of our nation's production ultimately depends upon the values our nation upholds.

''The new populism holds high a redeeming light for the U.S. economy and the world.''

—GEORGE GILDER, Author, *Wealth and Poverty*

''Richard Viguerie is as concerned with the ramifications of historical events as with the events themselves . . . those who look for shallow, short-sighted analysis will find Richard Viguerie more than challenging. On the other hand, others, including myself, find him brilliant, insightful, and wisely prophetic.

''Richard Viguerie's insights into the populist aspirations of grass-roots Americans should be required reading for all serious conservatives.''

—DR. RONALD S. GODWIN, Vice President, The Moral
　　 Majority

''The American free enterprise system is the greatest consumerist, populist movement in history.

''Liberals use populist rhetoric to sell socialist programs. Unfortunately the conservative often fails to understand that he espouses the ultimate populist position. Therefore, he often fails to communicate his message to the right groups in language they can appreciate.''

—HON. PHIL GRAMM, Member of Congress (Texas)

''In the past, it seemed that the only involved vocal activist groups were those of the '60s. Now, we see a new uprising in which a once silent voice has become clear and strong. The middle class of America, working blue and white collar Americans all, is involving itself in political activities because of its growing dissatisfaction with what has been happening to our country and where our country has been headed for years."

—HON. ORRIN HATCH, U.S. Senator (Utah)

"The elections of 1980 were a triumph for populism. Those who felt that big government, big business, and big labor should relax their hold on national decision making and let common sense prevail suddenly found that the country agreed with them. The challenge for the future is to translate this opportunity for meaningful self-rule into accomplished deeds."

—HON. PAULA HAWKINS, U.S. Senator (Fla.)

"The great majority of the people are patriotic, detest communism, and want to see America strong economically, militarily and morally; if they are silent it is only because the big media muffle their message."

—REED IRVINE, Chairman, Accuracy In Media (AIM)

"I consider myself a populist which I define as optimism about people and their willingness to respond to economic incentives as well as their ability to best control their own and their families' destinies. Above all, I am a populist because I believe in freedom and democracy, that it works, and that it is the true legitimate government for all mankind.

"Honest money is a populist, blue-collar, middle-class, bread-and-butter concern.

"Populism is basically the idea that you can trust people to make the right decisions about their own lives and about the country."

—HON. JACK KEMP , Member of Congress (N.Y.)

"The average American has felt that his destiny was in the hands of forces too big and too powerful for him to control or even significantly influence. Richard Viguerie's 'new populism'

offers the hope that man's future can be wrested from the hands
of big business, big government, and big labor and returned to
the hands of the individual where the framers of our constitution
intended it in the first place."

—DR. D. JAMES KENNEDY, Founder, Coral Ridge Ministries

"This book provides a timely look at a subject which should
be of interest to every conservative. The populist movement is a
response to many of the same concerns which trouble free market
conservatives."

—REED LARSON, President, National Right to Work Committee

"Richard Viguerie points out quite effectively that the new
conservatives are proponents of reform, not defenders of the status
quo. His is the new populism of the American dream. Viguerie's
book is indispensable for those who would understand the future
of American politics."

—LEW LEHRMAN, Chairman, Citizens for America

"The idea that unites contemporary conservative populists is
a sound one, that is: that civil government must always serve and
never tyrannize over a people. But the voice of the people is not
necessarily the voice of God. Thus, to succeed, contemporary
conservative populism must be under the God of scripture, or
like all those who attempted to build their houses apart from the
Lord, this effort too will be predestined to failure and destruction."

—JOHN LOFTON, Staff Columnist, *The Washington Times*

"Populist-oriented conservatism is a strong hope for advancing
the conservative cause. However, many conservatives, while ar-
ticulating populist sentiments, miss the mark because they really
don't understand the attitudes of working people. There is an
anti-liberal majority in America—but a good portion of that majority doesn't endorse a libertarian economic agenda. Conservatives need to talk down to earth, not theory. We need to reach
people in their kitchens. We need to take them where they are

and lead them to a conservative opportunity society.''
—CONNAUGHT MARSHNER, Director, Child and Family
  Protection Institute

''[Today's populists have] a keen sense of dismay with a federal court system seemingly hell-bent on imposing outlandish edicts on society.''
—JOHN MCCLAUGHRY, former assistant to President Reagan

''In 1980 under President Reagan's leadership the Republican Party confounded the stereotype and campaigned as the party of the blue collar worker, the shopkeeper and the small businessman. We talked of jobs, of individual saving, of individual investment—and our equal, across-the-board cut in tax rates for people was a central ingredient to that effort. It was precisely this 'populist' appeal that helped the President and the GOP win the hearts of an overwhelming majority of voters in November.''
—DEAR COLLEAGUE LETTER, May 4, 1982, signed by
  HON. BOB MICHEL, Member of Congress (Ill.)
—HON. JACK KEMP, Member of Congress (N.Y.)
—HON. TRENT LOTT, Member of Congress (Miss.)
—HON. DICK CHENEY, Member of Congress (Wyo.)

''The new populism is essentially the old democracy: that is to follow, rather than manipulate the will of the people, to rely on their intuitive wisdom rather than the program of a governing elite. . . .

''This requires a faith in the popular will difficult to find among professional politicians, academicians or journalists. They disdain the political instrument of populism—the referendum, the initiative, and other expressions of direct democracy.

''The elitist approves of bankers appointed for 12-year terms to the Federal Reserve board to control our money and lawyers appointed for life to the federal judiciary to control our lives.

''To opt for elective judges and a weakened central bank is the essence of populism.''
—ROBERT NOVAK, Syndicated Columnist

"Richard Viguerie's 'New Populism' correctly observes that the real battle in America today is not between Republicans and Democrats, but one which has greedy establishment elite using the tax process to prey on the working people of our nation."
> —HOWARD PHILLIPS, National Director,
> The Conservative Caucus

"The new conservative populism is fascinating but schizophrenic—genuinely populist on cultural and anti-institutional grounds, but unpopulist in its support for themes like the gold standard and Calvin Coolidge-type tax cuts. Its success or failure will be an important chapter in 1980 politics.

"America is the most populist nation in the world, and win, lose, or draw, the new conservative populism has the promise of being a fascinating chapter in the unfolding politics of the '80s."
> —KEVIN PHILLIPS, Syndicated Columnist

"Regretfully a small elite has often frustrated the will of the majority of the American people. Will the populist revolt be necessary to restore the voice of the people?"
> —DR. M.G. (PAT) ROBERTSON, President,
> Christian Broadcasting Network, Inc.

"In the Talmudic times, Rabbis instructed public officials who were in doubt as to the correct policy: 'Go and see what the people are doing.' This expresses what today we would call the populist insight: there resides in the good sense of the common man a sense for rectitude, wisdom, and conscience.

"Of course, we must be on guard against faddism, but the people frequently are far ahead of their 'leaders' and less prone to follow intellectual fashion. A good illustration of this is to compare the economic and political theories of academic authorities and the intuitions of ordinary people. I would be happier to 'see what the people are doing' than to listen to most professors."
> —RABBI SEYMOUR SEIGEL, Professor of Ethics and Theology,
> The Jewish Theological Seminary of America (on leave);
> Executive Director, U.S. Holocaust Memorial Council

"We cannot leave conservatism just to the country club set. If our populist movement is to survive and grow, we will have to continue to appeal to the values and beliefs of working people, as we did so successfully in 1980.

"We must articulate the frustrations and respect the common sense opinions of our farmers, clerks and blue-collar workers. If we ignore them, we are lost."

—HON. STEVE SYMMS, U.S. Senator (Idaho)

"Conservative populism is a hybrid amalgamation of generally accepted principles of limited government, free enterprise, strong national defense, and traditional fair values, richly blessed with a dose of common sense, from ordering people free from the infection of Northeastern Liberalism, special corporate interests, and moral relativism.

"Fairness is a big issue to blue collar workers. They don't mind wealthy people getting theirs. They just want to be sure it isn't at their expense. The Reagan administration has made a lot of mistakes here."

—PAUL WEYRICH, Director, Committee for the Survival of a Free Congress (CSFC)

"I believe the populist movement offers hope for the country. It is, at its heart, the voice of the people. That's government at its best."

—REV. DON WILDMON, Executive Director, National Federation for Decency

11 / 100 Ways To Make America Great Again

It won't be easy and it won't happen overnight, but Americans can make America great again.

In peace and in war, we have always risen to the challenge. We did it in the Great Depression and we did it in World War II. We can do it again.

I don't believe America is finished, or washed up, or ready for the dumping ground of history. And most Americans don't think so either.

All we have to do is pinpoint the real problems facing us and start working together to solve them.

So far in this book, I've shown how the elite establishment produced the economic, social and international mess in which we find ourselves today. The really hard thing is suggesting how to make it right again.

I have some suggestions and some solutions, based not only on my own thinking but on the study and analysis of dozens of populist experts in every part of our society.

We call for economic action, for social action, and for international action.

Our goal is a more prosperous America, a happier America, a more secure America.

And always, our first concern is not simply how to solve

a problem, but how to solve it in a way that is best for the people.

For example, we propose reducing the personal income tax to a maximum of 10 percent, not just because it will balance the budget, but because the people are being crushed by taxes.

We propose taking away the driver's license of drunk drivers, not simply to reduce the number of highway accidents, but to eliminate the terrible suffering of fathers and mothers, brothers and sisters who might lose a loved one because of a drunk driver.

We endorse the High Frontier concept of knocking down Soviet nuclear missiles, not just because it is more cost effective than our present system, but because it is a more humane way of defending ourselves than the current policy of MAD—Mutual Assured Destruction.

From the Declaration of Independence down to the present, our government and our society have rested on the solid foundation of the will of the people. Some Americans have forgotten that. We new populists haven't. It's the key to our program for making America great again.

I. ECONOMIC SOLUTIONS

Cutting Taxes

Let's begin with one of the most important issues of all—taxes. Our present tax system punishes working, discourages saving, takes away the income of hard-working Americans, and wastes it on useless federal programs.

Here are the basic elements of a sound and sensible tax policy for America:

● Establish a flat 10 percent tax rate on personal income with a $2,000 per person exemption from taxation. It's estimated that such a flat rate would produce the same revenue as the present tax code because people would report all of their income instead of concealing part of it as many do today. Even more important, people would start investing their money in productive ways and stop seeking non-productive tax shelters, many in other countries.

● Abolish the capital gains tax. We are the only industrial nation in the world that taxes capital gains.

● Eliminate taxes on IRA's (Individual Retirement Accounts). People's retirement savings should not be taxed. By increasing savings through things like an IRA, we increase the amount of money available to banks and other institutions to loan money to their customers to buy cars, houses and appliances as well as to expand their businesses.

● Persuade states to reduce their property taxes. Passage of Proposition 13 in California and Proposition 2 1/2 in Massachusetts forced state legislatures to take action. Similar citizens' groups proposing lower property taxes should be formed if state legislatures will not act.

● Eliminate any Social Security benefits for non-U.S. citizens or foreign workers here in the U.S. as illegal aliens.

The Gold Standard

America should go back on the gold standard. We need a solid measurable base for our currency and our economy. It is a fact that when Richard Nixon took America off the gold standard in August, 1971 (for basically the first time since 1792), he touched off the most inflationary 10 years in America's history.

Amnesty for Tax Cheaters

I favor a one-time amnesty from criminal prosecution for those who have cheated on their income tax. However, in exchange for this amnesty, the cheaters must settle their old accounts with the IRS, paying all civil penalties and interest on all past due taxes.

Supporters of tax amnesty estimate that as much as $80 billion could be recovered from people who otherwise would be afraid to admit their cheating.

Cutting this Budget

Cutting taxes will force the Congress to reduce the bloated federal budget. But we populists have some idea about where the budget should be cut.

(1) We're now spending about $260 billion a year on our national defense. And we're not getting anywhere near our money's worth. Here are some things that need to be done about defense spending:

● Prevent Members of Congress from trying to buy votes by approving new military bases not needed for our national defense. Billions of dollars have been wasted on bases from coast to coast as politicians and defense contractors have demanded a piece of the military pork barrel.

● Require competitive bidding and make better use of the Pentagon's spare parts system. Did you know that the Pentagon has paid $36.77 for a $1.08 machine screw, and $44 for a 17-cent light bulb?

● Stop subsidizing cut-rate groceries and other goods for active duty and retired military. Many people in uniform are making more money than millions of civilians. Raising prices to cover the full cost of military commissaries would save $750 million a year.

(2) No more federal money for political organizations. It's high time to stop funding homosexual, pro-abortion, anti-nuclear, radical feminist, thousands of liberal groups whose aims are not those of most Americans.

(3) Reduce U.S. support of the United Nations to the same level the Soviet Union pays. Why should we contribute twice as much as Moscow? We are now paying $1 billion a year for an organization in which, according to U.S. Ambassador Jeane Kirkpatrick, our influence "is trivial."

(4) Do away with revenue sharing that enriches already rich communities like Westport, Conn., and Palm Springs, California. At present 39,000 local governments receive checks from Uncle Sam through revenue sharing. Elimination of this program would save the American taxpayer about $5 billion. How can the federal government "share" with local governments when the U.S. government has annual deficits of $200 billion and there is nothing to share?

(5) Cut out corporate pork barrel projects like the Clinch River breeder reactor, located in Tennessee, which will cost $3 to 8 billion. If the giant energy companies want this new reactor so badly, let *them* pay for it, not the American taxpayer. Senator Howard Baker of Tennessee has been trying for years to get this pet billion-dollar project of his past the Congress.

(6) Eliminate federal funding for National Public Radio and the Corporation for Public Broadcasting, which underwrites public television. Estimated savings: about $172 million per year. NPR has been the ideological platform of the far-left since its founding.

(7) Stop building unneeded federal buildings like the $67 million one in Boston that has been unofficially named the "Tip O'Neill Federal Building". One federal official concluded that the 11-story, 793,000 square foot building could not be filled even if the government vacated *all* its leased space in Boston. We must stop funding these unofficial monuments to liberal politicians.

(8) Reduce our foreign aid program by at least 50 percent. At present we are spending $12 billion a year on economic, technical and other kinds of assistance to foreign countries. Estimated savings: $6 billion.

(9) Do away with the Synthetic Fuels Corporation. This is the boondoggle to end all boondoggles, a $14.9 billion program to pay Big Energy to develop alternative sources of fuel. Given their recent sky-high profits and the continuing high price of oil, why should the American taxpayer subsidize the oil companies now?

(10) Reduce the food stamp program by at least 50 percent. The food stamp program has soared from $462 million in 1962 to nearly $12 billion in 1983. Stamps have been used to buy filet mignon, fancy desserts, and tickets in state and local lotteries. The food stamp program is a prime example of a well-meaning welfare program turned corrupt. Estimated savings: $6 billion.

(11) Eliminate the public housing program, which now costs nearly $10 billion a year. From 1965 to 1979, the Department of Housing and Urban Development spent more than $76 billion to help provide decent housing for every American. At the end of that period, millions still lived in substandard housing. The answer to America's housing problem does not rest in more federal programs, but in lowering federal taxes and cutting federal spending, which will lower interest rates, so that builders can build and buyers can buy new homes.

(12) Eliminate the U.S. contribution of $8.4 billion to the International Monetary Fund. The IMF is a godsend to bankrupt countries and big banks, but it's a bad deal for the American taxpayer. We should stop guaranteeing risky loans by U.S. banks to foreign countries that cannot or will not pay what they owe.

(13) Do away with community development block grants. Originally intended to help the poor, these grants have been used by middle class cities and towns able to pay for their own development. Estimated savings: $3.5 billion.

I am looking forward to reading the new book by Donald Lambro, author of *Fat City*, whose articles in *Conservative Digest* and elsewhere have alerted so many to how Washington wastes our taxes. And I urge you to get a copy of the recent report issued by J. Peter Grace and his task force on the waste in our government from the Government Printing Office, 732 N. Capitol St., N.W., Washington, D.C. 20401. The Grace report pinpointed about $115 billion that could be saved each year.

Two Constitutional Amendments

The only sure way to bring federal spending and taxing under permanent control is through a constitutional amendment. The political pressures are such that even the most well-meaning President or Member of Congress is frequently unable to overcome the demands of those who want a solution *now* without regard for the consequences *later*.

I support the following constitutional amendments:

1) The Balanced Budget/Tax Limitation Amendment, which passed the Senate in 1982 but was defeated in the House because of opposition by Speaker Tip O'Neill and other big spenders. The Amendment would require the Congress to submit a balanced budget each year, and limit any increase in taxes to the national income growth in the prior year. The limit is waived in time of war.

2) A line item veto over the federal budget. The governor of every major state has line item veto power, permitting him to veto individual items in the legislature's budget. The President does not, although every President since Ulysses S. Grant has requested it.

National and State Referendums

Over 20 states have a referendum process which allows the people to propose a new law for consideration on the ballot. We should have the same process at the national level to allow a majority of the people in at least three-fourths of the states to propose a new law, or repeal an existing one.

Eliminating Local Regulations

The federal government is not the only government that has grown too big. State and local governments have increased their budgets, their taxes, and their intrusions into the lives of all of us, especially the small businessman.

State and local government agencies should abolish those laws, regulations and red tape that prevent small businesses from going about their business. An example of what I am talking about is occupational licensing. In New York City, taxi licenses cost $70,000. In Washington, D.C., they're $200. The result is that in New York City, you have too few cabs and too high charges. In Washington, you have plenty of cabs and reasonable charges.

Such regulations have hurt the very people they were supposed to help—minority Americans. It is a fact that New York has mostly white cab drivers while Washington has mostly black cab drivers.

In Wisconsin, women who have been embroidering clothing in their homes have been ordered to stop—they are in violation of U.S. labor laws. New York state forbids all "homework" unless the state gives special permission after "proper study". Other states allow homework only if the worker buys a license costing as much as several hundred dollars.

We should be encouraging, not discouraging, men and women in their homes and in their offices to show the kind of initiative that is the backbone of our free enterprise system.

Two-Year Budget

The present system of annual budgets just isn't working. The federal government should adopt a two-year budget cycle, as proposed by Marvin Stone of *U.S. News & World Report*, to eliminate the last-minute crises that engulf the government at the end of every fiscal year.

Congressional Staffs

Congressmen have been allowed to create their own mini-empires on Capitol Hill. Congressional and committee staffs should be sharply reduced.

Merit Pay

The principle of merit pay should be applied to government employees. At the same time, the firing of government employees should be made easier along the lines proposed by Donald Devine, director of the Office of Personnel Management.

Helping Savings

Savings enable people to make future plans like college for children, a new house, a new business, a vacation to a special place. Savings also enable banks and savings and loans institutions to lend money for business and pleasure. If it weren't for savings, we'd all be in trouble.

We should, therefore, be doing all we can to encourage savings, including:

● Raising the tax-free contributions homemakers can deposit in IRA's (Individual Retirement Accounts).

● Abolishing taxes on savings and dividends. The United States has the lowest ratio of savings to earnings of any major industrial nation. One big reason is that the government taxes our paycheck and then taxes the interest on our savings. No wonder so many Americans have joined the underground economy whose annual income is now estimated at over $300 billion.

Davis-Bacon

The Davis-Bacon Act, a long-out-of-date Depression law, should be repealed. It has artificially increased wages, raised prices, caused inflation, and produced fewer construction-related jobs.

Stop the Double Dipping

I want to end this section on suggested economic solutions with a comment about the federal retirement system, which pays $14.7 billion in benefits every year.

Populists believe in equal and fair treatment for every American. But federal employees are getting special treatment, especially in the area of their pensions.

Government pensions should not be given COLAS (Cost of Living Adjustments) which exceed those of the private, non-government sector. The average federal employee will pay $33,600 into his retirement program and can expect to receive, on average, $672,000—predicated on earnings of $24,000 a year for 20 years and his living and receiving benefits for 20 years after retiring.

II. SOCIAL SOLUTIONS

Victims' Rights

For too long in this country, the courts paid more attention to the criminals than their victims. Liberal do-gooders talked loudly about the responsibility of society to help the criminal, but softly if at all about the responsibility of society to the victims. But lately the scales have begun to tip the right way.

Thirty-six states have created victims' compensation programs to force criminals to repay some of the medical costs and lost income. In February, 1983, the President's Task Force on Victims of Crime urged all states to undertake such programs.

We endorse their recommendation, but it doesn't go far enough. We urge:

● A compensation program to make the criminal repay most if not all of the medical costs and lost income.

● Adoption by every state of so-called Son of Sam laws, named for multiple murderer David Berkowitz, that lock up proceeds from books and other ventures to satisfy claims by victims or their survivors. Only 15 states have such laws.

The important point in all this legislation is that it is the criminal and not the taxpayer who'll pay the victims.

As the *Wall Street Journal* has commented, "Much about the moral fiber of a society can be learned from the way it deals with crime." We have been compassionate, yes, but too often toward the wrong person. As between the rights of the criminally accused and the rights of potential victims, we must give priority to the rights of potential victims.

Stopping the Revolving Door

The majority of criminals serve only part of their terms (many are only put on probation), and the nationwide rate of repeat offenders is an alarming 65 percent. We have got to stop the revolving door through which the habitual criminal passes so easily and so often.

A major cause of this revolving door justice has been the Supreme Court, which has gone far beyond the Constitution and common sense in such cases as *Mapp v. Ohio*, 1961, where it ruled that if the police make even a technical mistake, evidence cannot be used. In *Miranda v. Arizona*, 1966, the Supreme Court said the police must tell the defendant he does not have to say anything and that he is entitled to an attorney. Even the slightest breach of these rules will result in a ruling for the defendant.

As a result, murderers have been set free, drug pushers released, and the convictions of rapists overturned.

The solution: courts must be required to observe what is called the good faith rule—if officers acted in good faith, evidence can be used. Likewise, confessions should not be dismissed because police mispronounced a word.

The insanity plea should be abolished so that criminals like John Hinckley won't be out on the streets in a few years.

The defense argument of diminished capacity due to alcohol or drugs should not be allowed.

In addition, there should be bail reform, especially denying bail to the habitual offenders.

Parole policy should be changed. It should not be given automatically, but only to those who by their record warrant it.

Plea bargaining should be denied to career criminals. Justice would be better served if the criminal knew beyond doubt that he will serve the term he has been sentenced to.

I believe in maximum jail sentences including life imprisonment for murder. But I do not favor the death penalty. I am a Christian, and I believe that the teachings of Christ are clear that you cannot kill a human being as punishment for a crime.

Nor do I think that justice is served if the book is thrown at everyone who comes before a judge.

Most first offenders for non-violent crimes, especially those with a wife or husband, and/or children, should be sentenced to work in community programs which require participation in service programs on weekends and full restitution to their victims.

Prisons and Prisoners

America's prisons are overcrowded because population and crime have increased. In 1981, the U.S. prison population was 369,009, an increase of 12 percent over the previous year.

Some conservatives have called for building more prisons. Some liberals have urged shorter sentences and the use of minimum security facilities rather than prisons. Both miss the point.

The solution lies in reducing crime, not in increasing the number of our jails, either of the maximum or minimum security kind.

No one can take any real satisfaction in putting a human being behind bars, unless he has proven beyond any reasonable doubt that he is a threat to society and belongs there.

We must make sure that the right persons are put in prison and that they stay there if their crime and their record justify it. I believe that prison should be reserved for those who are dangerous and those who, although not violent, are incorrigible.

Prison officials should be given more control over prisoner behavior. Much of their authority has been stripped away by liberal courts and liberal decisions. As a result, in too many places, prisoners run the prisons, producing violence and homosexuality. This must be stopped. It is wrong, it is immoral, it is a perversion of justice to subject people to physical violence and rape in jails.

Drug Use and Abuse

Drug abuse in the United States continues to be a major social problem. Of all criminal activities, the sale of drugs is probably the most profitable.

Most of the heroin, cocaine and marijuana on America's streets comes from foreign countries. The United States has been too lenient in dealing with overseas suppliers of drugs.

Columbia, Bolivia, and other countries should be given notice that unless they act to halt the massive export of drugs to the United States, we will reduce our aid and trade with them.

Drug paraphernalia laws should be adopted and enforced in all 50 states.

Life sentences with no parole should be made mandatory for those convicted on more than two occasions of dealing in illegal drugs.

Racketeering statutes which allow law enforcement officers to confiscate all of a drug dealer's property should be adopted and enforced in all 50 states.

Illegal Aliens

More than 500,000 illegal aliens enter the United States every year. Our legal admissions exceed those of all the other nations in the world combined.

Sen. Alan K. Simpson of Wyoming calls uncontrolled immigration "one of the greatest threats to the future of this country." He's right.

I want to help my brothers and sisters in every country. But if America accepts 10 million illegal aliens in the next few years (which would almost certainly happen if Central America goes communist), we will be strained to the economic breaking point. And our ability to stop the communists from conquering the world would be seriously reduced.

We can help our fellow brothers and sisters best by helping poor countries to become economically strong through adoption of our free enterprise system. There will then be no reason for them to seek a better life here—they will already have it in their homelands.

Taiwan, Singapore, and South Korea are all once-under-developed nations that are examples of what can be done with the right economic system and sufficient help and guidance from a developed nation like the United States.

In the meantime, we must control our borders. One practical approach is to prohibit the hiring of illegal aliens. Legislation has been introduced under which employers hiring illegal aliens would face fines of as much as $2,000, plus injunctions and contempt citations. In addition, we should:

● Establish a ceiling on all legal immigration of 425,000 per year, about the level of recent years, excluding refugees.

● Make it easier to police immigration. U.S. ships should be allowed to stop and turn back ships carrying people without proper documents.

As we struggle with this problem which is both a moral and an economic one, I can't help asking myself: Could it be that many wealthy people want illegal aliens as a source of cheap labor?

Drunk Driving

Nearly as many Americans died on our highways in the years 1981 and 1982 as were killed in Vietnam. 51,500 died in motor vehicle accidents in 1981, and 46,000 died in 1982. In both years, about one-half of the deaths were alcohol related.

On the average, about three Americans are killed and 80 are injured by drunk drivers every hour of every day.

Many states have begun to fight back. They are impounding vehicles driven by habitual offenders, bringing civil or criminal charges against those who serve drinks to drunks, and forcing drunk drivers to work for a public agency to help pay the costs of their cases. All this is not enough.

● Persons convicted of drunk driving should lose their licenses for one year.

● Persons convicted of drunk driving while their licenses

are revoked should be subject to confiscation of their vehicles, if they are the owners, and given a mandatory six months in jail, if they are not.

● Drunk drivers convicted of killing someone should receive a mandatory jail sentence at least equal to what they would receive if they were not drunk.

● The minimum drinking age should be raised to 21 in all states.

● Railroad employees should be barred from drinking for at least 24 hours before working. A 1982 poll of railroad employees showed that 19 percent were "problem" drinkers. That's 19 percent too many if they're responsible for the lives of others.

Homosexual Rights

Homosexuals have rights, but they do not have *more* rights than the rest of us.

They have a right to their own life, liberty and the pursuit of happiness, but they do not have a right to intrude upon our lives, our liberties, our pursuit of happiness.

"Gay" life as promoted by homosexual radicals is not an alternative life style. It is a defiant denial of the basic human instinct of procreation and the central tenets of our Judeo-Christian faith.

I strongly oppose "gay" rights legislation. I feel we should have the right not to hire, work with, rent to, or live next to a homosexual, or an adulterer, or a sexually promiscuous heterosexual, if we so choose.

Divorce

Seventy-nine percent of divorced fathers do not support their children. Twenty-five percent of American children are living with only one parent—an increase of 68 percent in the last 12 years.

One major reason for these shocking figures is that too many states have passed so-called "no fault" divorce laws, making divorce too easy. These laws should be revised to (1) make divorce more difficult, and (2) place more emphasis on the welfare of the children involved rather than the question of which adult gets the house and the car.

I also agree with Congressman Dan Marriott of Utah, who has recommended that there be required classes in junior high and high school, not on sex education but on parenting, marriage, and family responsibility.

Two Constitutional Amendments

Since 1973 and the Supreme Court decision of *Roe v. Wade*, there have been an estimated 15 million abortions in America. That is, 15 million babies have been killed. Abortion has become the law of the land. *This killing must stop.* We desperately need a constitutional amendment protecting the right of the unborn to be born, and we need it now.

"In God We Trust." It's on our currency, but it's not allowed in our schools. Thanks to Madalyn Murray O'Hair, a militant atheist, and the Supreme Court, voluntary prayer is not allowed in our public schools. We need a constitutional amendment allowing our children to pray to God before they begin their school day.

Welfare Reform

Reform is needed to bring runaway spending under control.

Medicare and Medicaid should be based on proven need. Food stamps should be replaced by commodities.

The Aid to Dependent Children program should be reformed: (1) a recipient must identify the father of the child, (2) failure to support a child should be made a crime, and

(3) payments should be limited to no more than three children except in the case of a legally married woman who has been divorced or abandoned.

Pornography

Local governments seeking to limit and ban pornography have repeatedly been overruled by the courts. Liberals, through the courts, are frustrating the will of the people.

In 1977, Congress voted unanimously to ban child pornography. But not a single conviction has resulted, despite the existence of a billion dollar business in our major cities. We know child pornography contributes to the shocking fact that more than 50,000 children disappear every year and are never heard from again.

The Congress and state legislatures should rewrite their anti-pornography laws, toughening them up and making sure that they result in putting these people out of business and behind bars where they belong.

Confirmation of Federal Judges

Federal judges should be made accountable to the people. All federal judges, including those of the Supreme Court, should be reconfirmed by the U.S. Senate every 10 years.

Politicians' Special Privileges

It's time for Congress to apply the laws of our nation to itself as well as to the American people.

In 1776, we fought a revolution against taxation without representation. Today, we are confronted with representation without taxation.

There must be an end to such special Congressional privileges as tax-paid junkets (most of which are vacations) and special tax breaks not available to other Americans.

Tax Credits and Deductions

Parents should have the right to choose the school for their children. But our tax laws work against those parents, often of modest means, who want to send their children to a private school.

We should allow the use of vouchers or tuition payments to private schools, including church schools, below the college level to be tax-deductible.

We should promote merit pay for teachers.

Busing

I support a constitutional amendment forbidding the use of busing for the purpose of producing so-called racially balanced schools. Such an amendment is favored by the overwhelming majority of black and white parents.

Quotas

Quotas and "affirmative action" in education and employment are insulting to minorities. They assume blacks, Hispanics and others cannot make it on their own but must be given special privileges. We need lower taxes and better schools, not more affirmative action and quotas.

National Day of Prayer

I call for a National Day of Prayer and Fasting, led by the President and top government and private sector leaders, to be held on the Sunday before Thanksgiving each year.

III. INTERNATIONAL SOLUTIONS

Peace and Freedom

I am concerned with bringing peace and freedom and prosperity to all peoples. It's immoral to let 1.5 billion people live under communist slavery. As a Christian, I cannot stand by and let that happen. The establishment's policy of trying to "contain" communism or engaging in a policy of "live and let live" with communism (meaning detente) is immoral. If you believe in containment or detente what you are really saying is that the communists can keep the 1.5 billion slaves they have if they will just leave you alone.

We need weapons to defend ourselves. But we must *never* allow weapons to become an end in themselves. They are just a way of bringing and keeping peace and freedom for every man, woman and child on earth.

The Truth About Communism

We should increase the Voice of America budget by at least $1 billion to bring the truth to people living under communism.

We should focus massive world-wide media attention on the evils of communism. We should call upon those people who have lived and suffered under communism to tell the truth about communism.

We should highlight the Soviet use of chemical weapons against the people of Afghanistan. We should urge the mass media to visit Afghanistan and assist them, if necessary, in getting in contact with the freedom fighters there.

Aid and Trade With Communists

We should stop all economic aid, loans and trade with all communist countries. This is a serious recommendation not lightly made. We cannot do business with nations and governments that systematically crush human beings. We must take a stand against such suppression, and we must take it now.

We should close all American ports to all ships from communist countries.

We should revoke fishing rights for all communist vessels in American waters.

There should be no scientific, cultural or athletic exchange programs with communist countries.

We should allow only as many communist personnel in this country as they allow us in their country. For example, the Soviet Union has about 400 percent more people in the U.S. than we have in the Soviet Union.

The United Nations

We should close down the U.N. headquarters in New York City. This will remove from the U.S. over 1,000 communist spies presently working in various communist delegations at the U.N. But that's not all the communist spies in America.

According to the FBI, over 3,000 officials of communist countries work out of about 180 offices in the United States. At least one-third of those officials are spies.

All of these spies should be shipped back to their communist "paradises" without delay.

As for the U.N. itself, wherever it lands—Geneva is a likely place—we should reduce our payments from the present 25 percent of the U.N. budget to the level paid by the Soviets, about 11 percent. Frankly, I question whether we should give anything to the UN, when you consider how often its members vote against us and for the Soviets.

American Aid

If countries want to have a socialist system, that is their right. But American taxpayers should not be asked to finance socialism—a system of economic distribution that doesn't work, except with our help.

Private U.S. banks should be forbidden to loan money to foreign countries unless they understand (1) they cannot look to the U.S. government to bail them out if the loans go bad, and (2) they cannot list such loans as assets in their reserve requirement under Federal law.

Freedom Fighters

We should openly give economic aid and arms and military training to the Afghan freedom fighters and to the anti-communist groups in Mozambique and Angola as well as the "contras" in Nicaragua.

Top government officials including the President should meet publicly with leaders of movements opposing communist military actions. For example, we should help Afghan freedom fighters get a wide TV audience for their heart-breaking story of how the Soviets are torturing women and children and spraying entire villages with poison gas.

We should stand up for our friends and allies whether they are small like Taiwan and Israel or big and strong like Great Britain and West Germany.

American Troops Overseas

We can save the American taxpayer billions of dollars by reducing the number of American troops in Europe and the Far East by at least 50 percent. This should be done over a period of 10 years or so. Such a phased withdrawal would force Western Europe and Japan to take a greater and fairer share of their defense burden.

Japan and Western Europe are taking jobs from Americans by not spending as much money on defense as we do. We're now spending about six percent of our GNP on defense; most Western nations spend only three percent of their GNP, and Japan spends about one percent.

Military Spending

I'm opposed to increasing our military spending as long as we're following a two-faced foreign policy.

Before I would support any increase in the defense budget, I would want two things:

1. President Reagan and his administration would have to communicate clearly to the American people that the Soviets are at war with us and explain clearly why we need to spend $260 billion a year on the military.

2. President Reagan and his administration would have

to stop helping the Soviets. There would be no more grain deals, no credit, no financing of loans, no selling of high technology, no building of hundred-million dollar truck factories, no more aiding and abetting the enemy.

High Frontier

We should adopt High Frontier as official U.S. policy and get behind it 100 percent. High Frontier is the non-nuclear, anti-missile defense program being urged by Lt. General Daniel O. Graham, USA-Retired. It is opposed by some Pentagon generals and defense contractors with vested interests in current weapons. President Reagan has endorsed High Frontier, but he should back up that endorsement with the same kind of commitment that put an American on the moon.

The Monroe Doctrine

We should enforce the Monroe Doctrine everywhere in Latin America as we did in Grenada. Enforcement would include increased support for the anti-communist forces in Nicaragua and the pro-American government of El Salvador.

We should work harder through the Organization of American States (OAS) to prevent communist subversion in Central and South America.

Removing Castro

We should undertake a combined political/economic/psychological campaign to remove Fidel Castro as dictator of Cuba. For nearly a quarter of a century, we have permitted Castro to export communist revolution and terrorism throughout Latin America and even into Africa. The time is now to take appropriate action to eliminate the Castro cancer from our hemisphere.

Republic of China

We should formally recognize the Republic of China on Taiwan, establishing full diplomatic relations with our longtime ally. As for Communist China, I predict it will accept our action after a lot of public threatening. Communist China needs us far more than we need it.

Foreign Intelligence

We should put the Central Intelligence Agency back to work. We should allow covert and overt operations against enemies of the United States and the Free World. Given the widespread and effective work of the Soviet KGB and other communist spy networks, it is insane to prevent the CIA from doing the job for which it was created.

Captive Nations

We should adopt an active policy of liberation throughout the world. We should encourage liberation movements in Eastern Europe, the USSR (where half the people now are not Russians, but of other nationalities), in China, in Cuba, in Afghanistan, in Vietnam, and elsewhere. We should provide these people with material as well as psychological assistance. We should keep promoting Captive Nations Week, which falls the third week of every July. Moscow hates this annual reminder of its aggression against weak nations and its oppression of the 1.5 billion people who live under communism.

The Voices of America

We need to expand dramatically the broadcasts of not only the Voice of America, but of Radio Free Europe, Radio Liberty and Radio Marti as well. Much of their equipment dates back to World War II, their hours of operation are limited, the number of their languages is inadequate. We have a revolutionary message of love, peace, freedom and prosperity to tell, but we are letting the Soviets drown us out.

World Peace Through Strength

We should declare a World Peace Through Strength Week each year, with every free world legislature adopting such a resolution.

Non-Negotiables

We should stop negotiating what is not negotiable, including the Law of the Sea Convention, the New International Economic Order, and other anti-American Third World ideas which are not in our national self-interest. Standing up for our rights, without apology, will strengthen world respect for the U.S.

Conclusion

These are some of my solutions, populist solutions, for making America great again. They touch the heart as well as the mind. They are based upon what people can accomplish.

They spring from my strong belief that God has put all of us here on earth to help each other.

I believe there is almost nothing we cannot do if we set our minds to it and follow God's laws.

Let us resolve to work together to make this nation and world a better place, a freer place, a holier place.

Let us commit ourselves to life, liberty and the pursuit of happiness for all.

12 / 'Good People'
A Problem, Too?

Do you feel that the election to the presidency of a person who agrees with you on all important public issues, together with a like-minded Congress, will provide the solution to most of America's problems?

After much reflection, I have concluded that it would not.

In taking control of the important aspects of our lives, the establishment has botched it badly. Most of us, however, must share a major part of the responsibility.

It would not be fair to blame all of our personal, community and material problems on the establishment.

Our problems can be directly attributed to the breakdown of moral and ethical consciousness, and with it, the movement away from obedience to God's laws.

Writing in the *Washington Monthly* of February, 1982, Robert Kennedy's daughter, Kathleen Kennedy Townsend, cited examples of official attitudes which, to her, suggested "that this country is in serious trouble, and that the crisis, at bottom, is a moral one." She continued:

"We've lost something at the core of our national character that once acted to shape our behavior. We've lost our sense of virtue."

"Discussion of moral values," she wrote, "makes most

liberal Democrats nowadays uneasy.''

In the euphoria of victory and economic prosperity following World War II, Americans began *to emphasize their own personal pleasure before their responsibilities to their brothers and sisters and therefore to God.* Continuing this trend gave birth to the ''Me'' generation of the 60s and 70s. While there are signs that many Americans are turning back to God, larger numbers are still pursuing values clearly in violation of His laws.

There is a natural law which I believe strongly. Simply stated: We will get back in like kind that which we've done.

The law is founded in religion and in science. The Bible in both Old and New Testaments says it many ways:

> **''. . . all that you wish men to do to you, even so do you also to them; for this is the Law . . .'' (Matt. 7:12)**

> **''For what a man sows, that he will also reap.'' (Gal. 6:7)**

> **''Cast thy bread upon the running waters, for after a long time thou shalt find it again.'' (Eccl. 11:1)**

For those who rely less on the Bible and more on science, there is Sir Isaac Newton's 3rd Law: ''For every action there is an equal and opposite reaction.''

The sum of all of this is that we can expect direct consequences from our actions—whether individually, or collectively as a nation.

In the eyes of the Lord, the sins of a people lead to the eventual destruction of their nation, as seen in the destruction of Sodom and Gomorrah.

> **''Virtue exalts a nation, but sin is a people's disgrace.'' (Proverbs 14:34)**

Have you considered that you could be as responsible for America's problems as the homosexual pimp on New York City's 42nd Street?

Many times people think that their life is in good shape because they are not an adulterer, and they don't drink or gamble.

The truth is, however, that most of us are doing things which have consequences that may be as bad as the offenders of some of God's better known laws.

The establishment has been able to take control of our lives because of the inactivity or wrong activity on the part of the law abiding 'good people.'

Lets look first at our inactivity.

Are you aware of the need to conserve and protect our environment? We are here as stewards of this world. We do not have the right to use in a wasteful manner the things in God's world. We have a responsibility to preserve and protect what God has given us for our use.

Do you turn out lights when they are not needed and minimize your use of heat and air conditioning?

Do you visit old people, the lonely, the sick, the bereaved, the dying?

Are you helping poor people, orphans, troubled children?

In your selection of books, magazines, movies and TV shows, do you set examples for your children and others?

Are you registered to vote? Do you vote in every election? Are you aware of the views of the candidates or are you voting blindly for party or a personality?

Do you give generously of your time to elect candidates who share your views and values? Remember, freedom is not free; it was purchased for our use at a great price by those who came before us.

Do you pray frequently for peace and freedom for all people of good will?

Do you give a day's work for a day's pay? Do you take

pride in all honest work?

When you can do so safely, do you stop and give assistance to someone whose car is broken down or who has a flat tire or is burdened down with packages?

Now that we've taken a look at some of the things we may not be doing—let's take a good look at some of the things Americans have been doing and if we are honest, most of us will find ourselves a number of times.

Between 1960 and 1982, there were in America:

- 18.5 million divorces

- 23 million users of illegal drugs

- 18 million babies killed by abortion

- 189 million serious crimes reported

- 9.5 million illegitimate births

- 550,000 deaths and 14,300,000 injuries from drunk drivers

    And in 1982:

- An estimated 20 percent of all taxpayers cheated on their income tax

- An estimated 60 percent of employees cheated their employers by thefts of goods, improper use of postage meters, falsely claiming sick days, etc.

- Over $10 billion was spent on sex magazines and books (including *Playboy*) and X & R rated movies

- An estimated 10 million practicing homosexuals

- 5 million alcoholics

If you still haven't found yourself in any of the above categories, perhaps you're one of the millions who:

● Cheat on their spouse and commit adultery (*The Hite Report*, found that 72 percent of men married two years or more had had extramarital sex.)

● Charge higher prices because insurance will pay the bill;

● Inflate your insurance claim because the insurance companies "have plenty of money"

● Demand high price supports for farm products (milk, corn, sugar, peanuts, etc.) causing others, including poor people, to pay much higher food prices

● Expect other taxpayers to pay for your children's college education by getting a low interest government loan

● Accept unemployment compensation paid by your employer when you voluntarily go on strike

● Drive after two or more drinks

● Claim a business deduction for a meal or a trip for non-business purposes

● Are quick to rush to court (or threaten to) over relatively minor matters

● Tell or laugh at off-color, ethnic or racist jokes

● Want taxpayers to pay for the leg you broke while skiing because you volunteered for the military during peace time

● Expect taxpayers to contribute $6 dollars for your government retirement for every $1 you put in

The point is that those who are messing up our country and our lives are not just the elite, the establishment, the obvious sinners, publishers of pornography, drunks, thieves, and welfare cheats.

A major part of our problems come from "God-fearing," "law abiding," church-going, "good citizens" who watch Dallas, Dynasty, Saturday Night Live, afternoon soap operas, drive after several drinks, don't declare all of their income for tax purposes, and who insist on government (taxpayer) subsidies.

If we all think about the little things we do that may not be exactly honest or moral, the list would go on and on.

In a *Time* Magazine article January 24, 1983, Frank Trippett wrote: "Americans are used to thinking that law-and-order is threatened mainly by stereotypical violent crime. When the foundations of U.S. law have actually been shaken, however, it has always been because ordinary law-abiding citizens took to skirting the law.

"It is painfully apparent that millions of Americans who would never think of themselves as lawbreakers, let alone criminals, are taking increasing liberties with the legal codes that are designed to protect and nourish their society."

The article went on to list examples of how 'good people' violate the law: bicyclists who ride as though two-wheeled vehicles were exempt from all traffic laws, litterbugs, those who play radios loudly in public places, smokers blind to no smoking signs, people who spit on sidewalks, and drivers who double park, exceed the 55 mile an hour speed limit, or run red-lights.

An October 18, 1982, *Wall Street Journal* editorial said in discussing crime: "But government doesn't bear the full responsibility. Community leaders, educators, the clergy and family heads must stress the importance of individual responsibility and self worth. Perhaps then more people will show respect for their fellow man."

As the character in the comic strip, *Pogo*, once said, "We have met the enemy and he is us".

In 1835, Alexis De Tocqueville said: "America is great

because America is good. And America will cease being great if America ceases being good.''

De Tocqueville understood the cause and effect of natural law.

However, it is obvious to me—and I hope to you—that sometime within the past 35 years we Americans have lost much of our moral focus.

Usually, we can easily and quickly see the faults of others, but seldom do we clearly see our own shortcomings.

During the 200 year history of our nation, we have been less than perfect, and we've suffered for it.

However, I believe, our faults and shortcomings as a people are far worse today than they were 50, 100 or 200 years ago. Few of us can escape responsibility for our share in the present decline of our country and our civilization.

Consequently, our problems are so great that many serious thinking people feel our economy may collapse, or that we are destroying the environment for our heirs, or that the world may run out of food, or that we may destroy the world in a nuclear holocaust.

Edmund Burke once said: ''All that is necessary for the triumph of evil is for good men to do nothing.''

I suggest that an adjustment to Burke's statement is appropriate: ''If people do wrong, then evil will triumph.''

We are turning our eyes, our minds and our hearts away from a universal truth if we think that the election of good men and women will solve our problems while we continue to have high levels of pre-marital sex, adultery, homosexuality, abortion, immoral movies and TV shows, alcohol abuse, illegal drug use, income tax cheating, excessive personal and government debt, and large numbers of middle class and wealthy people (farmers, dairymen, businessmen and bankers) expecting the taxpayers to give them subsidies and healthy people who refuse to seriously try to earn a living.

The history of the world is the story of societies collapsing under the weight of decadence and greed—Rome, Greece, the Byzantine Empire, Ancient Egypt, Babylon and Mesopotamia, among others.

In order to regain our greatness and once again become the beacon for all mankind, we must recognize and overcome not just the obvious qualities of evil but also its subtleties.

There are over 81,500 rapes or attempted rapes reported in the United States each year. More subtle, however, are the far more numerous instances of discrimination against women, or against blacks, or against anyone else because of his or her race, religion or creed.

This insidious problem is far more harmful to society than is imagined.

As Christ taught, we must look beyond the letter of the law and into the heart of the law. We must begin to look into, and examine, our hearts and minds, as well as our actions, for insidious offenses against the spirit.

We must guard against being honest in the flesh but a thief in spirit.

It is wrong to rely upon the machinery of government to attend to the needs of our less fortunate neighbors rather than personally seeking out and attending to those needs on a one-to-one basis. For as the scripture says: "Each of us must look to others' interest rather than our own, and our attitudes must be that of Christ." (Phil. 2:4-5)

Individually or collectively, we are not smart enough to figure out how to get out of the mess we're in. Our only hope is to ask and receive God's help. With His help, Communism, government and personal debt, crime, illegal drug use, alcoholism, and all other problems will disappear overnight.

As I said earlier, the election of a President and Congress that agrees with you almost 100% won't solve our problems.

Probably the only way we can save America is by the

election of a great leader as President who believes in and understands God's law. This could provide a small window of opportunity for us to change our future if he would dedicate his Presidency to this proposition. Individually, and in groups, we should pray for God to send us this leader.

Obviously, a President can't make us do the right things. But, because of his or her position and access to the media, the President can use his office to help raise our consciousness on those things that contradict the will of God and contribute to our problems as individuals and as a nation.

Not only is it impossible to change our country by merely electing a good and right thinking person as President, but also political activity is futile as long as the populace at large is in a state of moral decay.

The choice is ours: we can stay on a course bent on certain destruction, or we can choose to live up to our potential greatness, choosing good and doing good, and reaping the harvest of goodness.

13 / Whither Populists?

Before the decade is out, average Americans will rise in revolt against the concentration of power in the hands of the establishment. The most powerful force in U.S. politics will be a movement that identifies with and speaks for our nation's most neglected class: people who work for a living.

For too long our government has ignored the interests of the average citizen. All he asks from his government is that it defend the shores, build the roads, catch the criminals, and educate the children. All he asks for a lifetime of hard work is a peaceful retirement and a better life for his grandchildren.

Yet, at the direction of the establishment elite, the worker's own government has chosen to meddle in his life—threatening his family by allowing criminals to walk the street, taking his wages and spending them on caviar parties for the International Monetary Fund, and busing his kid across town to a school where prayer is about the only activity that isn't tolerated. He is justifiably angry.

I believe that conservatives, as heirs to the populism of Thomas Jefferson, will harness that anger and turn it in a constructive direction. I believe that a party of the people—perhaps rooted in one of the existing parties, perhaps not—

will arise in a manner entirely consistent with the traditions of American democracy.

Already there have been skirmishes in the larger political war to decide the direction of the coming populist revolt. In recent elections, smart politicians in both major political parties have maneuvered to identify themselves with the populist impulse. In 1980, Reagan's Republicans were identified with the populist cause. In 1982, Democratic candidates across the nation, particularly in Texas and the South, identified themselves with populism.

• Texas Attorney General Mark White ousted William Clements from the governor's office by highlighting Clements' insensitivity to the problems of the working class. Clements' statement that he "didn't know of any housewife who is qualified" to be on the state board that regulates utilities was just one example of that insensitivity. (Clements should have considered the example of Paula Hawkins, a homemaker who served so well on Florida's utility commission that she was later elected to the U.S. Senate.)

• George Wallace returned to office in Alabama by attacking the country-club Republicans who dominated his opponent's campaign. When the GOP held a $1,000-a-plate fundraiser, Wallace countered with a $2-a-plate hotdog lunch ("and anyone who's out of work can eat free!")

• In Arkansas, Bill Clinton returned to the governor's office by shedding the image that had led to his 1980 defeat: Yale-educated, an early supporter of George McGovern, with a wife who didn't use her husband's last name. By 1982, he was able to present himself as more concerned about the problems of average Arkansans and his wife had become Mrs. Clinton.

By 1983, politicians in both parties had begun to use the term "populist" to describe their own orientation. On February 23, 1983, Congressman Tom Harkin (D-Iowa) announced the formation of a Congressional Populist Caucus that included 14 liberal Democrats, most of them from the Midwest. Meanwhile, a group of House Republicans, most of them relatively young, have taken up the banner of what is called (for lack of a better term) "populist conservatism." Among the leaders of the populist conservative group are Congressmen Jack Kemp (R-N.Y.), Newt Gingrich (R-Ga.), and Phil Gramm (R-Texas).

It is not surprising to see some politicians taking on the "biggies" in the banks, the corporations, the legal profession, the media, and the government. They sense that a tidal wave of populist sentiment is heading our way.

Their effort to seize and direct the frustration of the common man is not unprecedented even in recent history. Less than a decade ago, a group of conservatives, most of them populists, sought to build a coalition to roust the establishment from the halls of power.

In the aftermath of Watergate, when Ted Kennedy was the leading Democratic candidate for president and Nelson Rockefeller was the Republican vice president, a number of political activists sought to unite the so-called social conservatives of the Democratic Party with the so-called economic conservatives of the GOP. The social conservatives were mostly people who had supported George Wallace in 1968 for non-racist reasons. The economic conservatives were members of the Taft-Goldwater-Reagan wing of the Republican Party.

A large number of activists supported the idea of a new third party as the vehicle for that coalition. William Rusher, the publisher of *National Review* magazine, wrote a book called *The Making of the New Majority Party* in which he outlined an "Independence Party" that would "do to the Republican Party what the latter did to the Whigs: namely, replace it in *toto*." At the 1975 Conservative Political Action

Conference, a Committee on Conservative Alternatives was formed to research the prospect of a third party.

The idea of a new party was abandoned primarily because of the opposition of the one leader at the time who could have welded such a coalition—Ronald Reagan. Reagan made it clear that his effort to seek the presidency would be confined to the Republican Party.

In February 1977, Reagan explained his position. "I cannot agree with some of my friends who have said this nation needs a new political party," he said.

"I respect that view and I know that those who have reached it have done so after long hours of study. But I believe that political success of the principles we believe in can best be achieved in the Republican Party. . . . Rather than a third party, we can have a new first party made up of people who share our principles."

Reagan said the party he envisaged "will not, and cannot, be limited to the country club big business image that, for reasons both fair and unfair, [the GOP] is burdened with today. . . . If we are to attract more working men and women of this country, we will not do so simply by 'making room' for them, but by making certain they have a say in what goes on in our party."

Following Reagan's lead, anti-establishment activists turned their energies toward changing the Republican Party. Most of them channeled their efforts through the Reagan presidential campaign, although a few supported Congressman Phil Crane (R-Illinois) or former Texas Governor John Connally. When, after a virtual six-year campaign, Reagan secured the GOP nomination, it seemed that the "new first party" he spoke of would finally come into existence.

In 1980, it was the Republican Party that appeared to be more representative of working Americans, more concerned about the problems of Joe Lunchbox than the Democrats were. The Republicans' nominee for president ran as a citizen-politician independent of the "Washington buddy system" that caused so many of our problems. He spoke of the U.S. involvement in Vietnam as a "noble cause" and expressed doubts about the theory of evolution.

The members of the establishment laughed at Reagan's "gaffes" but the people saw him as someone who shared their values. Like working Americans who are stereotyped as rednecks and Archie Bunkers, Reagan was ridiculed for his beliefs by a self-righteous band of elitists with access to the major communications media.

At the Republican National Convention, the theme of which was "family, work, neighborhood, peace, and freedom," Reagan accepted the presidential nomination, departing from his prepared text to "confess that I've been a little afraid to suggest what I'm going to suggest. I'm more afraid not to. Can we begin our crusade together in a moment of silent prayer?"

"Afraid"? Millions of Americans knew what he meant. Reagan was "afraid" because prayer is an activity that can earn you the scorn of the nation's elite. Apart from invoking God's guidance, the call for prayer sent a message to voters: Here at last was a presidential candidate who would stand up to the establishment. It got across the point that Gerald Ford had tried to make in his acceptance speech four years before: *It is from your ranks I come and on your side I stand.*

Alas, like Jimmy Carter, the man he defeated and replaced, Ronald Reagan turned his back on the populist cause. The working people of this country were eager for dramatic change when, in 1976 and 1980, they voted for the candidates they believed would break up the concentration of power in the hands of the elite.

Both Carter and Reagan promised to provide new leadership by recruiting accomplished people from the private sector into the government and not relying on the "old boy" network. Carter's 1976 campaign manager, Hamilton Jordan, said, "If, after the inauguration, you find Cy Vance as secretary of state and Zbigniew Brzezinski as head of national security, then I would say we have failed."

Contrary to their promises, both presidents came to rely on advisers with Ivy League graduate degrees and uncallused hands. Few officials of either administration worked their way through state universities, labored on assembly lines, or started their own small companies before rising to important positions in the worlds of business and politics. (One of the rare exceptions is Gerald Carmen, who established an auto parts business in New Hampshire in 1959, built it into a statewide chain, and as of this writing serves with distinction as head of the General Services Administration.)

In selecting persons to staff their administrations, Carter and Reagan used criteria generally accepted by the establishment. In the establishment view, the most important qualifications for government service generally include one or more of the following: a degree from an Ivy League school, membership in a prestigious law firm, experience as a top executive in a large corporation, and service in a previous administration. By those standards, few people with working-class backgrounds have any chance of being selected.

There is nothing wrong with a person who meets such "qualifications." But a person's basic values and his ability to triumph over adversity should be considered as well.

After years in which the best-qualified small business people, craftsmen, graduates of state universities, etc., have been excluded from consideration for most important positions, it must be assumed that we would be better off if that reservoir of talent had been tapped. Given the experience of the last 50 years, people who have "pulled themselves up by their bootstraps" from the lower classes are probably more qualified than those born to wealth and power.

The elitists howl every time a person without establishment credentials achieves success. When a Ronald Reagan or a Harry Truman is elected to the presidency, they constantly question his intellectual ability, while a political leader who attended Harvard or Yale is considered intelligent no matter how disastrous his policies or distorted his values.

Consider the way Judge William Clark has been ridiculed repeatedly by the establishment. Robert A. Kittle wrote in the January 18, 1982, *U.S. News and World Report* that "when William P. Clark came to Washington as the President's choice for the No. 2 job in the State Department, he was ridiculed for confessing that he knew virtually nothing about foreign affairs. Earlier in his career, as a Reagan nominee to the California Supreme Court, Clark was derided as unfit for the judiciary because he had dropped out of college, flunked out of law school and, on his first try, failed the bar examination. . . .

"In each instance, the 50-year-old Clark ultimately won over many of his critics by showing an ability to master new turf rapidly. On the California court, his conservative judicial opinions earned him grudging praise from many of those who originally belittled his intellectual caliber. In his 10 months at the State Department, he proved to be a skillful administrator and an adept diplomat."

Judge Clark is a person who can do many things well. There are many more like him across the country, people who could do an outstanding job in a high government position but who are excluded from consideration because they don't have establishment credentials.

Another problem with the way in which people were selected to work in the last two administrations was that, after assuming office, Carter and Reagan neglected some of the groups most important to their election. For example, both candidates appealed strongly to born-again evangelical Protestants, but few members of that group received appointments to high government positions. The issues important to them were given lip-service and the key people in each administration had little time for them.

The only person well-known as a born-again Christian to serve in the top level of the Reagan Administration, Interior Secretary James Watt, was forced to resign in October, 1983.

Perhaps the main reason for that mistreatment of some of Carter and Reagan's most important supporters is the fashionable Washington prejudice against evangelicals, whom a *Washington Post* columnist recently referred to as "Bible-thumping bigots." Bigotry against evangelicals is expressed most vocally by such groups as Norman Lear's "People for the American Way," but intolerance pervades our national media. For example, the Christian faith of Secretary Watt was lampooned in the *Doonesbury* comic strip in a manner that, had the "joke" been directed at the beliefs of Jews, would have branded the strip's artist as anti-Semitic at best. Recently columnist Art Buchwald "humorously" referred to Watt as a "born-again nerd."

Whatever the reason, there is no doubt that, with rare exceptions, conservative Christians have been given short shrift in the last two supposedly-populist administrations. Jimmy Carter didn't consult seriously with his evangelical supporters until late in his presidency. And Lou Cannon wrote in his book *Reagan* that, when a White house aide was asked what the new Reagan Administration planned to give the Moral Majority "and its allies," the aide replied, "Symbolism."

Since, according to the ABC News-Lou Harris survey reported November 11, 1980, "The white followers of the TV evangelical preachers gave Ronald Reagan two-thirds of his 10-point margin in the election," it is astounding that a White House aide would make such a statement. But, in fact, symbolism (and not much of that) is all conservative Christians received in return for their votes. They are brought

to the White House occasionally for picture taking opportunities, but they are almost never included in the decision-
making process.

The treatment of conservative Christians is just one example of how hardcore loyalists are treated by the Reagan
White House. Even Ralph Nader has commented that officials of the Reagan Administration have "disdain" for the
conservative groups that helped elect the President. In August, 1982, Nader said the groups had been "thoroughly
replaced by representatives of business who seem to have
as little time for debates on school prayer and abortion as
they do for promoting the government's health and safety
functions."

When, after campaigning as outsiders, Carter and Reagan
governed as traditional presidents of their respective parties,
many people felt betrayed and retaliated on election day.
We saw the results in the great Republican shifts of 1978
and 1980 and the Democratic victory of 1982.

As this is written, President Reagan has not announced
whether he will seek reelection. Time is running out for him
to revive his support among the less privileged citizens. If
he continues to be identified with Wall Street rather than
with Main Street, he can be reelected only if his opponents
are likewise insensitive to working people.

The President may run again and the Democrats may
nominate Walter Mondale, another far-left candidate like
McGovern; thus, the voters' distaste for the Democratic
candidate might result in a Reagan victory. But, assuming
Reagan continues to be identified as a "rich man's president," a victory based on his being the lesser-of-two-evils
will mean continued Democratic majorities in Congress and
state governments. Reagan will have failed to end the Republicans' long-held status as the country's minority party.
His "coattails" will be as short as Nixon's were in 1972.

Ronald Reagan's failure to bring about a significant realignment of political loyalties is one of the great tragedies of recent history. If he had been able to forge a coalition of the type he described repeatedly during the mid-1970s, the Jeffersonian populist sentiments of the American people would have been translated into positive action. Instead of predicting future political events, this book would record the history of the Reagan Revolution.

Unfortunately, Reagan has been unwilling to reach out to Democrats and independents when it means sacrificing the support of Republican elitists. Mostly forgotten are dreams of forging a new majority party. In state after state, members of the establishment are at this writing gearing up to run the President's reelection campaign. If Reagan chooses not to run, the elitist's lock on the machinery of the GOP will be even stronger. After years of back-breaking work trying to push the Republican Party away from the country club set, populists are as far away from controlling the GOP as they ever were.

There is a clear lesson in the disappointments of the last few years: Populists cannot count on a single leader to rescue the nation from the disastrous policies of the establishment. While the populist movement will need strong leaders, there is no one individual in whom we should invest our hopes for the future, no "man on a white horse" who will lead us to the Promised Land.

Nor can we depend on either of the two major parties to provide the vehicle by which the people's voice will be heard. The Republican and Democratic Parties are too firmly grounded in the concerns of the well-to-do and the welfare state. The new populist movement must have a broad base of leadership nurtured over a period of years if it is ultimately to succeed.

With the right kind of leadership, such a movement can channel the people's frustration in a constructive direction that will enhance the liberty of all Americans. It will include:

• The Sagebrush Rebels: Westerners furious at a federal government that owns 86.5 percent of the land in Nevada, 89.5 percent of the land in Alaska, and 65.3 percent of the land in Idaho—a pattern of federal control repeated throughout the West. Isn't it about time that Washington let local people control their own resources?

• The alternative education movement: about 8 million people across the country who are educating their children in private schools or at home because of the deterioration of the public schools, or because they don't want the educational establishment indoctrinating their children on subjects like "value-free" sex and the nuclear freeze.

• Outdoor sportsmen: hunters and fisherman angry at "environmentalist" efforts to waste millions of acres of land by shutting it off from human contact.

• Anti-crime groups: people banding together to make the law pay more attention to the rights of the victim than the rights of the criminal. Groups like the Stephanie Roper Committee (she was brutally raped and murdered) in Maryland and Mothers Against Drunk Driving are springing up all over the country.

• Religious conservatives: Christians and Jews who want to stop pornography and curb sex and violence on television and in movies.

• "Gold bugs": advocates of gold-backed, inflation-proof currency—money that keeps its value.

• Gun owners: citizens who want to protect their constitutional right to own firearms. As a recent referendum in California proved, and the liberal Democrats in that state learned to their sorrow, this group has the potential to be one of the most effective forces in politics.

● "Ethnic" anti-communists: First-, second-, and third-generation Americans whose friends and relatives suffer under the yoke of communist tyranny in North Korea, Cuba, Eastern Europe, Afghanistan, Vietnam, and scores of other nations.

● The right-to-life movement: People who may or may not belong to formal right-to-life groups, but are determined to protect innocent human life from abortionists.

As time passes, the great coalition I describe will include young people who realize that they may never receive Social Security benefits, thanks to the bungling of the establishment. In the years to come, as new technologies give politicians entirely new types of businesses in which to meddle, the populist movement will attract whole industries whose workers want freedom from the interference of Big Brother in Washington.

To say that this movement will not depend on the leadership of a "man on a white horse" is not to play down the need for dynamic leaders. The success of any coalition depends largely on its ability to cultivate leadership that is both reasonable and charismatic. That leadership will come from a wide range of citizens' groups.

You can't beat somebody with nobody, it is said, so the movement will need to produce as soon as possible a spokesman who is a potential president. He or she may be someone who has never sought political office or whose name is unfamiliar to the general public as of 1983. The principal requirement is that the spokesman be a reassuring figure, someone who can convince the middle class that it is time to abandon the old leaders and the old coalitions and follow him or her to a new home in the populist movement.

Whoever he or she may be, the principal spokesman must be "one out of many," an individual more concerned about building a successful movement than with fame or personal power. The spokesman must have clear ideas on how to elect people to Congress and state governments, not just the White House. If a leader consumed with personal ambition were to dominate the new movement, it would be fragile and temporary, dependent on the success or failure of one individual. It must not be allowed to degenerate into just another presidential campaign vehicle, like most new parties.

Which brings us to an important question. Will the new populist movement take the form of a new political party?

If a new party were based on the ideas I have outlined in this book, it would not be a mere offshoot of the Republican Party or strictly a "conservative" party. With the right kind of leadership, it could avoid unnecessary labels and cut a path carefully between the Big Business Republicans and the welfare state Democrats.

It would be a party of the economic and cultural center of America, drawing from all segments of society that are victimized by the establishment. It could draw from the current major parties, from independents, and from the millions of Americans who don't vote because neither party gives them an acceptable choice. In the early days, at least, most of its leaders would be persons not tied to the existing parties—leaders of single-interest groups concerned with gun control, right-to-life, crime, pornography, prayer in our schools, and communism, as well as leaders of more broad-based groups.

Such a party would find a base in the South, where distrust of the national Republican and Democratic Parties remains high. It would have great appeal in most of the West, which, like the South, has experienced more than its share of abuse by federal bureaucrats.

So far, my description of the geographical base of the party sounds like "the Emerging Republican Majority" projected by Kevin Phillips in his book of that title. According to Phillips, American politics since the time of Andrew

Jackson has followed a basic pattern: power accumulates in the hands of an Eastern establishment; that establishment is overthrown by a coalition of the South and the West; the new governing coalition acclimates to the East, and the process begins anew.

Phillips' book, which despite its title is one of the best analyses of political trends ever written, describes the sort of coalition Nixon or Reagan could have put together but didn't. I believe the opportunity to build a majority coalition under the Republican banner has passed. Insightful though Phillips may have been, his blueprint for a realignment is not the one populists will follow.

I believe a new populist party must be based on more than just a theoretical outline or a plan to take advantage of demographic trends. To be a true national party, it must also appeal to people in the states where the original Populists were strong and where the Progressives and other anti-establishment parties had a measure of success. Other states may be targeted because of voting records that suggest a populist base.

North and South Dakota, Kansas, Nebraska, Oklahoma, Kentucky, Missouri, West Virginia and New Hampshire are all states where a populist party must take a stand if it is to succeed nationally. But it must have a presence in every state, in order to take advantage of unexpected opportunities.

It is difficult to design a master plan that will tell a political party where it will find success. Just one example will suffice: Twenty-three years ago, there were no Republican senators from the South; today there are as many Republican senators as Democrats in that region, and they provide the GOP with the margin by which it controls the Senate. Who could have predicted such a development? A new populist party might find pockets of support in all sorts of unexpected places.

Whether Ronald Reagan runs for reelection or not, there

is a strong chance that a populist political party will arise in time for the 1984 election. It is unlikely that the party would oppose Reagan, although it would run or endorse candidates for Congress and state and local offices. (If the Republicans were to nominate a Bush, Baker, or Dole, a new party will be involved in a presidential race as early as 1984.) Thanks largely to the third party efforts of George Wallace, Eugene McCarthy, and John Anderson, it is much easier to get on the ballot in all 50 states than it was a few years ago, despite the efforts of Democratic and Republican politicians to make the task more difficult.

Most polls show a large majority of the American people opposed to increased taxes, busing, trade with communists, quotas, and affirmative action, and more government involvement in our lives. The people support voluntary prayer in schools, a balanced budget, and getting tough on criminals. But neither major national political party has come up with a satisfactory response to the desire of the people for change in government policy on those subjects.

The GOP, the party that comes closer to agreement with average Americans, has been inflicted for half a century with an inability to take advantage of the gap between the Democrats and the people. It has won five of the last 13 presidential elections, but only twice in the last 27 congressional elections has it won a majority in the House of Representatives. Republicans have controlled the Senate only seven years of the last 53.

At the state level, the Republican Party has swung between being insignificant and impotent. At the end of October, 1983, the GOP held 15 governorships. Only 37 percent of state legislators across the country were Republicans.

Few, if any, political analysts think the Republican Party can improve its status in the near future. It is in such bad shape that, if I were a liberal, I would want it to remain the principal opposition to the Democratic Party. But it is dif-

ficult to understand why conservatives want to keep it around.
Sure, it is the party of Goldwater and Reagan, but it is also
the party of Weicker, Mathias, Baker, Dole, and Bush.

Perhaps the main reason for the reluctance to abandon
the GOP is fear of the unknown—fear that, no matter how
bad things are, a change could make it worse.

Another reason is that many elected and appointed Republican officials have a vested interest in keeping the GOP
alive, even as a permanent minority. A new majority coalition would be a serious threat to their continuation in office.

As John Sears, the former Reagan campaign manager,
once said, the GOP is like a fungus—it's sick, but you can't
kill it.

In today's political climate, the moderate/liberal Republican establishment that runs the Reagan White House could
not elect one of their own campaigning on their beliefs.
They can get to the White House only on the backs of
millions of contributors and volunteer workers who are part
of the populist wing of the party.

Members of the Republican establishment argue that the
populists, at least the conservative populists who call themselves Republicans, have "no place to go" and dare not
leave the Republican Party. They say to the conservatives:
If you don't do your usual job of rescuing the GOP by
providing 80 percent of the contributions and 90 percent of
the campaign workers, you'll end up with Mondale as president, and you wouldn't want that, would you?

It's like the story some parents tell their children: If you're
not a good little boy or girl, the bogeyman will get you.

The establishment Republicans scare populists into supporting their candidates with horror stories of what will
happen if his opponent is elected. Better Nixon, the devil
you know, than McGovern, the devil you don't know. Better
Ford, the lesser of two evils, than Carter. If you're not good,
Mondale, Kennedy, Humphrey, or Stevenson—whomever

conservatives fear most at the moment—will get you.

That argument will no longer hold. Conservative populists are tired of winning elections for Republican candidates only to be excluded from the decision-making process when those candidates win.

As Suzanne Garment wrote in the October 7, 1983, *Wall Street Journal*, "The moderates may find that they've won one too many battles if the conservatives really prove themselves willing to crash through the walls of the Republican Party structure to take their place in the wilderness."

Who knows? Perhaps one of the major parties will turn away from the elite that has controlled it for decades and a new party will not be necessary. But, as they say in North Dakota, I wouldn't bet the farm on it. I believe the resentment the people feel against the governing elite has created a huge reservoir of political energy that neither moderate nor liberal Republicans, liberal Democrats, nor radical leftists are capable of harnessing.

Responsible populists, unconcerned about the political label they may wear, have a chance to gain political power, to restore the traditional relationship between a democratic government and a free people.

Prudent people involved in the political process must recognize that we are in a transition phase with all the attendant instability and potential dangers. The political orthodoxy of the post-World War II period is being rejected.

Politics, like nature, abhors a vacuum. If the existing parties fail to respond, a new force will rush in. My fervent hope is that the resentment the people feel toward the governing elite will be turned in a constructive direction by the new populist movement.

I'm basically optimistic. I have seen the tremendous growth of anti-establishment forces over the last decade or so, and if that growth continues, the populist movement will not lack strong, responsible leadership.

The populist movement, whether as a separate party or not, will represent the just interests of working Americans and oppose the concentration of power in the hands of a few. It will fulfill a great American tradition. As Stephen D. Hayes wrote in the Winter 1980 issue of *Commonsense,* "The Founding Fathers designed the Constitution with a fear of over-concentration of power uppermost in their minds. The intricate balancing of the three branches of government reflects this fear. So does the designed balance, which some would argue has been irreparably disrupted, between the federal government and the state governments.

"The fear of centralized political power . . . can and should be taken to its logical conclusion: There is a danger when too much power of any kind is concentrated *anywhere.* It is not just the U.S. government but the basic fabric of American society which depends on a rather delicate balancing of competing interests, geographic sections, and various factions—all centers of power. Those who share this view carefully watch and try to hold in check, not only big government, but big business, big labor, and even (through indirect pressures) big media. For, in each case, the word 'powerful' can be substituted for the word 'big.'"

In this book, we have met the power brokers, the big boys, the guys who pull the strings. They are Big Business, Big Unions, Big Government, and their allies in the fields of education, the media, organized religion, banking, and the law. What we have discovered is that the members of the establishment are no more skillful, no more talented, no more intelligent than you or I; they have simply been in a better position to pursue their own ends at the expense of the rest of society.

We have met the enemy, and they are not us. (Or are they? See the chapter on "good people.")

We bear responsibility for the mess they make only if we let them get away with it. It is our duty to join with our fellow citizens to create a legitimate opposition to the elitist establishment, to develop an alternative consistent with American principles of government, and, finally, to govern well when the people come to power.

Against all the forces that manipulate the government to their own ends, the populist movement will speak for the individual—in William Graham Sumner's words, "the forgotten man."

". . . The Forgotten Man is delving away in patient industry, supporting his family, paying his taxes, casting his vote, supporting the church and the school, reading his newspaper, and cheering for the politician of his admiration, but he is the only one for whom there is no provision in the great scramble and the big divide. . . . He works, he votes, generally he prays—but he always pays—yes, above all he pays. . . . He keeps production going on. . . . He is strongly patriotic. . . . He is not in any way a hero . . . or a problem . . . nor notorious . . . nor an object of sentiment . . . nor a burden . . . nor the object of a job . . . nor one over whom sentimental economists and statesmen can parade their fine sentiments. . . . Therefore he is forgotten."

It is our job to make sure the forgotten man is remembered. Let's get to work.

14 / *The New Populism Will Prevail*

Remember *The Wizard of Oz?* Near the end of the movie, Dorothy, the Scarecrow, the Tin Woodman, and the Cowardly Lion return to Oz, to ask the all-powerful Wizard for the rewards he has promised them. Amidst smoke and flame, the Wizard appears as an immense, godlike image and his thundering voice fills the hall.

But then Dorothy's little dog Toto pulls back the curtain to reveal that the all-seeing, all-knowing Wizard is just a sideshow man with machines that make him seem great. Exposed at last, the Wizard points out to Dorothy's friends that the rewards they had sought—a brain, a heart, and courage—were already theirs. They didn't need to come to him, to bow down and follow the orders of the great Wizard. All they needed to do was look within themselves.

That story illustrates an important idea: that those who claim dominion over the lives of others are not special in any way, except that they are able to put on a good show of special effects. Otherwise, they are no better than those they seek to dominate.

Do not misunderstand me. The members of the establishment elite that I refer to are not evil. Indeed, some of them have worked all their lives for what they believe to be the good of society and many of their works have been good. They have built hospitals and libraries, financed medical research and the arts, and helped society in ways beyond number.

But they have no place telling you or me how we should spend our money or raise our children. Members of the elite have tried to use the power of government to impose their values on society, always "for a good cause," and the inevitable result has been failure.

Remember what happens when Toto reveals the Wizard of Oz for what he is—a charlatan whose superiority is an illusion? Dorothy exclaims, "You're a very bad man!"

"Oh, no, my dear," says the Wizard. "I am a very good man. I'm just a very *bad* wizard."

For the most part, the establishment elite is made up of very good men and women who happen to be very bad wizards.

In this book, I have discussed the establishment, and the ways members of the elite create the illusion that they are more intelligent and more wise than the rest of us. I have suggested some changes that can be made to take power away from the few and return it to the people.

Today's populists, in the tradition of Thomas Jefferson, seek to restrain the power of government. They want to prevent the government from granting special privileges to the few at the expense of the many. The modern populists have an advantage over the populists of the 1890s, who had little understanding of socialism because it had not been tried; today we know that a powerful central government can only increase the domination of the establishment over our lives.

There are still some who, in the name of populism, advocate a stronger government. Some who call themselves populists believe that government can be used as a tool to redistribute power "fairly."

But the lesson of history is that government does not operate "fairly." A government is run for the benefit of the people who run the government. At best, the liberal "populists" would substitute bureaucracy and regulation for wealth and prestige as the tools used by the powerful to maintain control.

The genuine populists of the 1980s want to reverse the flow of power to Washington, to give individuals more control over the decisions that affect their lives. Today's populists oppose the establishment's use of governmental power to further the objectives of big business, big unions, and their allies.

Conflict between the people and the elite is inevitable, because the establishment seeks to maintain the status quo. Because substantial change may mean the emergence of a new elite to challenge the old, the establishment tries to prevent change (and, failing that, to control its direction).

The establishment view is expressed by politicians who talk about the limits of growth, about how people are going to have to learn to live with less, about how our children's lives will be more difficult than our own. These politicians see a world slowly winding down, with mankind's greatest achievements already behind it.

On the other hand, populists see the future as a great adventure. Considering how we got from Kitty Hawk to the space shuttle in one lifetime, they wonder how far we will go in the years to come. To them, resources are not limitations on the progress of humanity, because they believe that mankind makes its own resources and that progress is limited only by imagination. A dynamic society, unburdened by the preconceptions and prejudices of the elite, is the goal of the new populists.

Impose a mindless orthodoxy on society, and you will see that society decay and, eventually, after untold suffering, it will collapse. But let each individual do what is right for himself or herself, and nothing is beyond your grasp.

As John Ciardi wrote:

Who could believe an ant in theory?
A giraffe in blueprint?
Ten thousand doctors of what's possible
Could reason half the jungle out of being.

For too long the establishment—ten thousand doctors of what's possible—have tried to restrict the people with shackles of status and political power.

They have told us that it's not possible to create an economy so productive that poverty can be eliminated. They have told us that it's not possible to free the world from the threat of communist domination. They have told us that it's not possible to restore the traditional morality that is based on the simple idea, *Do unto others as you would have them do unto you.*

Frankly, I've had it up to here with "experts" telling me what is possible and what is not possible. I think it's time to stand up and say what is plainly true: that the establishment elite are a burden on the people, dragging us down in an age when we have the potential of going to the stars.

And we're not going to take it any more.

We're going to raise a banner around which will rally all Americans and all peoples within whose hearts the fire of freedom burns. It will be a banner of bold, unmistakable colors—the colors of a new dawn of freedom.

More than 200 years ago, a great war was fought over ideas: the principles of the Declaration of Independence, that freedom is not only morally right, but absolutely necessary for a nation to achieve virtue and prosperity.

With those ideas guiding them, the American people brought down a government that denied them their rights and sought vainly to regulate their commerce for the so-called "common good.'' After the revolution, the people established a government that they hoped would protect their rights and leave them otherwise free to manage their own lives.

Today, it is our responsibility to join with our fellow citizens, to join together not as conservatives or liberals, Republicans or Democrats, but as individuals working together to restore the American Dream.

And we shall not allow ten thousand experts, ten thousand wizards, or ten thousand doctors of what's possible to stand in our way.

Afterword:

An Open Letter to Presidents, Present and Future

A President gets a lot of advice, most of it unsolicited.

However, unless the advice is from the high and/or the mighty, a President seldom hears it.

The average citizen has much that he would like to tell a President, but few ever get the chance.

I have met and talked to only one sitting President (Ronald Reagan), and then only briefly on a few occasions.

As with most Americans, however, hardly a day goes by that I wouldn't like to give the President at least one piece of advice.

So with the hope that some President or an important government official may stumble upon this chapter, I am going to unburden myself.

Level With The People—Give Them the Facts

It may be that a President has no more important task than to make sure that the people are well informed about problems facing the country now and in the years ahead.

This is normally the job of the communications media in a free society. But because America's media aggressively pursue the liberal agenda, most issues are not fairly presented to the American people.

For example, the media were solidly against America's

involvement in Vietnam in the 1960s and 1970s, as they now are against our involvement in Central America.

So when Lyndon Johnson, Richard Nixon, and Jerry Ford failed to tell the American people the seriousness of the threat we faced from the communists in Vietnam, the people did not understand the need to be involved militarily.

It is very difficult for people to correctly perceive a problem if they do not have most of the facts.

Do Not Allow Pollsters In The White House.

In a July 27, 1983, article in the *Wall Street Journal*, Irving Kristol said: "If I were President of the U.S. my first commandment to my staff would be: Thou shall not permit a pollster on the premises. The function of pollsters is to convert leaders into followers."

I strongly agree. A President (or any leader) should do what he feels is right without regard to whether it will help or hurt him among voters.

A good attitude for the President to have is to assume that he will only hold office for one term.

It has been said that the best Presidential reelection strategy is for a President to be a good President. I'm sure that's true, but it is hard to be a good President if one measures most decisions by how today's action may effect one's reelection.

Many people feel that politicians will say whatever is necessary to be elected or reelected. By not checking the polls constantly, a President will send a message to all concerned that he is trying to lead as best he sees fit, not according to which way the wind may seem to be blowing at a given moment.

Don't Overwork Yourself, Your Staff, Or Appointees.

One of the most serious mistakes a President and his aides can make is to work long hours regularly.

There is no evidence that a President who works 14 to 15 hours day in and day out is more successful than one who works eight or nine.

L.B.J., Nixon, and Carter had the reputations of working crushing hours, but few would make the case that their Presidencies were crowned with success.

Over the years I've noticed a common characteristic about airline stewardesses and stewards. Some are more pleasant than others, some are more attractive than others, some are younger than others, but all work hard.

And the same can be said about the White House staff at most levels, as well as about most of the President's top appointees and their staffs.

This is true whether they are Democrats or Republicans, liberals, moderates, or conservatives.

I think Presidents make a serious mistake by routinely working long hours and allowing their staff to do the same.

A person does his best work when life is balanced. A balanced life should include time for physical exercise, relaxation (such as non-business related reading or listening to music), seven or eight hours of sleep, a good diet, quiet time, quality time with family, prayer, and reading good spiritual books (beginning with the Bible).

Keep Your Promises.

Many people have a low opinion of politicians; one major reason, I believe, is because time and again politicians at all levels make campaign promises which, after they are elected, they seem to forget.

There is no justification for a President (or anyone) to lie. A President seen as morally strong will have much stronger support for his programs than otherwise.

If a President believes he must take a position different from one taken in the campaign, he should say so—and explain why his position has changed.

People will admire and respect a President or any other officeholder who treats them in an honest, forthright manner.

A politician loses his moral authority for leadership if he

changes his position and denies that he has done so, or ignores a campaign promise and says he hasn't.

Meet Regularly With People From All Walks Of Life.

Most Presidents have limited contact with people other than those at the top rungs of the establishment ladder. A President's day is usually spent meeting or talking with top aides, longtime close friends, or the wealthy and powerful—such as the heads of corporations, big unions, and Congressional Committee chairmen.

This means that a President receives a rather limited range of views on issues. The establishment has certain issues of concern, such as anti-trust legislation, government regulation of big business, defense contracts, import and export policies, etc.

Issues such as busing, crime, pornography, rape, tax cuts for the middle class, and the dangers of selling the Soviets militarily usable items are not on their list. So things not of interest to most of the establishment are seldom discussed in the presence of a President.

In an informed, relaxed atmosphere, a President should meet regularly with people from all walks of life—such as small businessmen, school teachers, farmers, local government officials, secretaries, salesmen, nurses, local law enforcement personnel, and social workers.

Keep Faith With Your Supporters,
Appoint Your Supporters To Important Jobs.

One of a newly elected President's great frustrations is his discovery that he can appoint a relatively small number of people to government jobs—6,323 out of a total of 2,950,000 non-military government employees.

There are always many more supporters who want jobs than there are vacancies.

Therefore, it is doubly important that most appointed positions go to a President's supporters. It is important that, in a democracy, large numbers of people participate as volunteers in any election campaign. When, as in the case of the Reagan Administration, those who worked for a President's election discover that the vast majority of important appointed positions are being awarded to people who did not support the President and his postions, they are understandably disenchanted.

A President must maintain the good spirits of thousands of people of shared ideology and interest if he expects them to spend their time, energy and money for his reelection. One way this can be done is for the President to invite them to large and small social gatherings. Another is for him to make from four to eight telephone calls a day to key people at the local level in politics, charitable activities, and religious organizations.

America has local ministers, state legislators, heads of local charity drives, and thousands of leaders in local unions and small business who must be given cause to believe that they are really part of the national scene. They must be convinced that their elected leader wants to know their views and hear their suggestions.

That is important for the President to remember. It is no less important for members of his Cabinet.

When a President or his subordinates appoint people to positions who hold views different from his own publicly stated views, great damage is done to the democratic process.

People have a right to assume that, when a candidate for any elected office, especially President of the United States, sets forth his views and his policies in a campaign, he will conduct himself and his administration accordingly.

Establish And Communicate Your Goals.

At the beginning of his term of office, a President should explain his objectives to the people. He should establish a reasonably manageable number of achievable goals, then communicate them to the nation.

Periodically, he should give the people reports on his

programs, policies, progress, and problems. He should seek the people's support, help, and prayers.

In the Spring, 1981, issue of *The Journal of the Institute For Socioeconomic Studies,* Dom Bonafede and Thomas E. Cronin suggested: "Presidents can make a vital difference by building popular morale, renewing the public's faith in the democratic system, defining critical problems and priorities, inspiring trust and confidence in national values and offering a vision for the future, as well as by the caliber of their appointments, their ability to forge supporting coalitions and their firm response to events."

"In fact," they said, "one of the incontestable reasons underlying Ronald Reagan's victory last fall, was that he exuded a contagious self-confidence. However much we fancy our system as a government by the people, we still are attracted by people who can make sense of the issues, who seem to have some new solutions and *who believe in themselves.* Where Carter complicated the issues and talked about the limits of the office, Reagan discussed the issues in a straightforward and communicable language (perhaps in too simple a way). Further, he projected a 'can do,' 'we can overcome,' 'I'm all right, we're all right,' 'we can tackle these problems together' attitude."

Teddy Roosevelt said he believed in using the Presidency as a bully pulpit. I agree that the Presidency affords a tremendous opportunity for a good person to lead the people in a righteous direction by telling them regularly what they should, and should not, be doing.

The most effective leadership, however, emerges and distinguishes itself through personal example. There is an old, very true, adage: "What you do speaks so loudly that I cannot hear what you say."

A great President must be morally strong, carry the courage of his convictions, be good to his family and the people. He must never lie, seek revenge, or level personal attacks upon those who may oppose him.

Give Generously Of Your Time And Money.

If a President's financial position permits him to serve without accepting his authorized official salary, he should consider doing so, and he should encourage his Cabinet officers to do the same. This could be a great symbol of sincerity and dedication to public service and leadership.

Another inspiration through leadership can come via a President's leading the people in prayer and fasting and visiting the sick, the dying, and the elderly.

What greater mark of leadership than adherence to *The Beatitudes?*

Appendix I / Action Steps at the Local Level

People all across the country are taking action and making democracy work. Two of the best known examples are the overwhelming passage, in 1978, of Proposition 13 in California and, in 1980, of Proposition 2½ in Massachusetts.

Proposition 13 cut property taxes by $7 billion dollars a year by limiting them to 1 percent of 1975-76 assessed valuations, and required a two-thirds legislative vote to impose any new state taxes.

Proposition 2½ cut Massachusetts property taxes by an average of 40 percent over several years, saving property owners $1.2 billion; cut automobile excise taxes 62 percent; and allowed renters to deduct half their annual rent on their state income tax returns.

Both campaigns to reduce the burden of taxes started at the grass roots, and were supported and won by the people against establishment forces: Big Government, Big Business, Big Unions, and their allies in banking, education, law and media.

There have been many more similar and successful campaigns across the country. Where people were united and determined to take back control of their lives they have overcome all the power of the establishment.

How? By utilizing local, county, or state level Initiatives and Referenda to pass laws that reduce taxes, balance state budgets, restrict or regulate abortion, stop pornography, fight crime, improve education standards and generally make the states, counties and cities more responsive to the will of the people.

On these pages I have set forth a number of suggested ballot items that may be used in an Initiative and Referendum campaign. You may think of others that may be more important in your state.

However, the important point to remember is: If you live in a state with the Initiative and Referendum process, *you* can use it to help take back control of *your* life.

POPULIST LEGISLATION THAT CAN BE PASSED UTILIZING STATE, CITY, COUNTY LEVEL INITIATIVE AND REFERENDUM PROCESS

● "To reduce taxes."

● "To provide for the election, rather than the appointment, of all judges."

● "To require judges to stand for reelection every seven years."

● "To require a vote of the people to validate the passage of new or increased taxes on either the state or local level."

● "To abolish the defense of 'temporary insanity' in criminal cases."

● "To require criminals to begin paying restitution to their victims as a condition of probation or parole."

● "To establish a 'crimestopper' program to pay rewards, from a fund established through voluntary contributions, to citizens who furnish information leading to the arrest and indictment of criminals for major felonies, especially involving drug trafficking and organized crime.''

● ''To prohibit the establishment of civilian review boards for police, unless authorized by a vote of the people.''

● ''To prohibit the use of state or local funds for abortions, except in cases when abortion is necessary to save the life of the mother.''

● ''To permit doctors and nurses to refuse to participate in the performance of abortions without losing their jobs or being discriminated against in any way.''

● ''To require medical personnel to give all necessary care to babies who survive abortions, rather than killing them or allowing them to die of neglect.''

● ''To require parental consent for minors to be able to obtain abortions.''

● ''To prohibit 'social promotions' in public schools, except for students with mental impairments or learning disabilities or with limited English proficiency.''

● ''To permit silent prayer or meditation in public schools.''

● ''To strengthen the authority of classroom teachers by giving them the direct authority to suspend unruly students.''

● '' 'Sunset' laws to require all state agencies with appointed members to automatically cease existence every 10 years, unless affirmatively renewed by law for another decade.''

● ''To require all state and local agencies to utilize clear, concise, non-technical language in all of their rules, regulations, forms, publications, and other documents.''

● ''Right-to-work laws, which prohibit discrimination against employees in hiring on the basis of membership or non-membership in a labor union.''

● ''To prohibit electric utility companies from charging more per kilowatt for users who supplement their electricity with wind-powered or solar-powered generating devices.''

● ''To repeal any land-use restrictions that prevent citizens from erecting solar or wind energy generating equipment on their own homes or businesses.''

● ''To permit a court in which an individual is sued by a state agency to order the state agency to pay the defendant's attorney's fees, upon a finding by the court that the state agency's suit was frivolous, unreasonable, or without foundation.''

● ''To require proof of automobile liability insurance to be presented when an individual purchases or renews license plates.''

● ''To increase the drinking age to 21 years.''

● ''To permit administrative suspension of licenses of drivers who refuse to take breath tests for blood level alcohol.''

● ''To revoke licenses of drivers convicted of homicide by motor vehicle.''

● ''To require suspension of a juvenile's drivers' license for any drug or alcohol related offense, regardless of whether it involved drinking.''

● ''To prohibit nudity or obscene activities in places where alcohol is sold for on-premise consumption.''

● ''To make it a crime to show X-rated films at public theaters or to sell hard core pornographic books, movies or sexual devices.''

● ''To ban from cable television systems films which portray explicit sexual conduct, erotic nudity, or violence with erotic overtones.''

Twenty-three states provide for the right of Initiative and Referendum. The specific requirements vary widely. Your Secretary of State or Attorney General can provide the details for your state.

Many towns and cities in states which, themselves, have no initiative and referendum process have processes of their own which allow citizen ballot measures. For city or county information on this matter, contact your city or county clerk or board of elections.

There are several methods you can use to collect the necessary number of signatures. Card tables may be erected in the malls of busy shopping centers with volunteers available to explain the proposal and solicit signatures on the petitions. Another technique is personal contact, door-to-door, in residential areas. Some successful petition drives have used direct mail to obtain the signatures.

Only about 15 percent of all attempts actually succeed in collecting the required number of signatures. Only about one in three that reach the ballot are approved by the people. But while the odds are long and the tasks are difficult, the process of Initiative and Referendum represents an excellent opportunity for hard-working populists to translate their philosophy into action.

Anyone interested in promoting the initiative and referendum process may get involved by contacting these organizations:

Americans for the National Voter Initiative Amendment, 3115 N Street, Northwest, Washington, D.C. 20007 (202-333-4846).

Initiative and Referendum Report, Free Congress Foundation, 721 2nd Street, Northeast, Washington, D.C. 20002 (202-546-3004).

Finally, if your state does not provide for the initiative and referendum process, you can attempt to remedy that condition with a state constitutional amendment.

Appendix II / A Game of "What If?"

In this book, I discuss the possibility that a new populist political party will be formed in the near future.

Steven Allen, a political scientist, recently gave me this projection of the way the votes might break down in a contest for the Presidency, with candidates representing the Democrats and Republicans, a John Anderson-type liberal party, and a populist party. He got these figures by feeding election returns from the period 1968–80 into a computer and designing a hypothetical model of a four-way race.

I don't vouch for the accuracy of this projection. After all, there are too many variables involved in any election, such as the personal qualities of the candidates, their home states, their running mates, and so forth. But it is interesting to see how one political scientist thinks the votes might split on a state-by-state basis. If a populist party is on the ballot in a future election, the popular vote percentage and the electoral vote might break down something like this.

State Electoral Votes	Percent of Total Vote			
	Republican	Democrat	Populist	John Anderson-type Liberal
Ala. (9)	18.7	21.7	**55.6**	4.0
Alas. (3)	18.0	26.8	**48.2**	6.8
Ariz. (7)	27.7	23.9	**40.8**	7.4

State Electoral Votes	Percent of Total Vote			
	Republican	Democrat	Populist	John Anderson-type Liberal
Ark. (6)	21.9	23.2	**50.2**	4.5
Cal. (47)	34.6	**35.0**	21.7	8.5
Col. (8)	30.1	27.3	**33.6**	8.7
Conn. (8)	33.8	**35.2**	20.7	10.1
Del. (3)	32.9	**33.0**	26.5	7.3
D.C. (3)	24.1	**53.9**	12.8	9.0
Fla. (21)	35.7	22.4	**36.2**	5.6
Ga. (12)	21.5	21.4	**52.7**	4.3
Haw. (4)	27.9	**32.7**	30.4	8.8
Ida. (4)	30.4	23.0	**40.2**	6.2
Ill. (24)	**36.7**	35.4	20.0	7.7
Ind. (12)	**36.2**	30.4	27.2	6.1
Iowa (8)	**36.4**	32.0	23.4	8.1
Kan. (7)	**35.7**	27.7	29.4	7.0
Ky. (9)	30.6	27.8	**36.8**	4.7
La. (10)	20.6	22.3	**52.7**	4.2
Me. (4)	28.9	30.6	**31.9**	8.4
Md. (10)	29.5	30.5	**32.5**	7.4
Mass. (13)	29.4	**40.9**	17.7	11.7
Mich. (20)	31.4	**33.7**	27.4	7.3
Minn. (10)	29.4	**33.3**	29.2	7.9
Miss. (7)	18.3	21.0	**56.5**	4.0
Mo. (11)	21.6	31.1	**41.6**	5.5
Mont. (4)	**33.0**	30.2	28.8	7.7
Neb. (5)	**37.6**	27.1	28.0	7.1
Nev. (4)	27.1	25.9	**39.8**	6.9
N.H. (4)	**32.9**	29.5	27.4	9.9
N.J. (16)	**35.7**	34.1	22.2	7.8
N.M. (5)	31.1	28.3	**33.7**	6.7
N.Y. (36)	34.1	**36.7**	20.9	8.1
N.C. (13)	28.9	24.7	**41.5**	4.8
N.D. (3)	**34.9**	28.7	28.7	7.4
Ohio (23)	**33.7**	32.9	26.5	6.8
Okla. (8)	29.6	24.6	**40.6**	5.1
Ore. (7)	**31.2**	30.0	30.3	8.3
Pa. (25)	**35.7**	35.5	21.6	7.1
R.I. (4)	29.4	**41.6**	17.2	11.4
S.C. (8)	24.6	23.1	**48.0**	4.2
S.D. (3)	**34.0**	33.4	25.2	7.2
Tenn. (11)	24.7	23.0	**47.8**	4.4

State Electoral Votes	Percent of Total Vote			
	Republican	Democrat	Populist	John Anderson-type Liberal
Tex. (29)	25.0	25.4	**44.9**	4.6
Utah (5)	20.3	19.4	**56.1**	4.1
Vt. (3)	**34.7**	32.1	21.3	11.6
Va. (12)	27.1	24.7	**42.2**	5.8
Wash. (10)	32.3	**32.4**	26.0	9.1
W.Va. (6)	28.1	30.9	**35.3**	5.6
Wis. (11)	**31.8**	30.3	30.6	7.1
Wyo. (3)	29.7	26.4	**36.7**	7.0
Total Electoral Vote	155	158	225	0

Index

Compiled by
Thomas J. Blumer and Brent L. Kendrick